M000309641

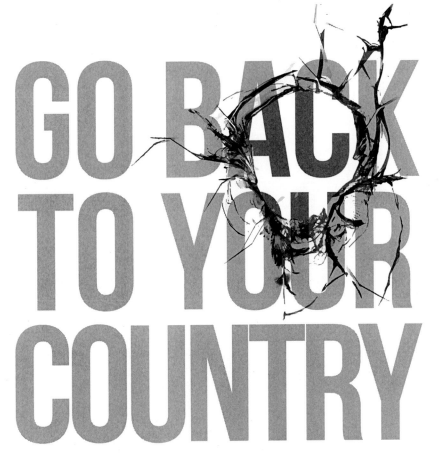

GO BACK TO YOUR COUNTRY

(OR STAY & DEFY ALL ODDS)

GO BACK TO YOUR COUNTRY

(OR STAY & DEFY ALL ODDS)

BY ISSA MUSHARBASH

LEGACY
INTERNATIONAL
PRESS

LEGACY
INTERNATIONAL
PRESS

Go Back to Your Country
(Or Stay & Defy All Odds)

Copyright © 2020 by Issa Musharbash. All rights reserved.

Written permission must be secured from the publisher to use or reproduce any part of this book, except for brief quotations and critical reviews or articles.

This is a work of creative nonfiction. The events are portrayed to the best of the author's memory. While all the stories in this book are true, some names and identifying details have been changed to protect the privacy of the people involved.

ISBN: 978-0-578-78002-3 (Paperback)

Cover Design by:
David Leonard
JungleCommunications.com

Printed in the Unites States of America

Published by Legacy International Press
177 Broadway
Bayonne NJ 07002

LegacyInternationalPress.com

Quantity Orders:
Special discounts are available on quantity purchases by corporations, associations, and other groups. For details, contact the publisher at the address above.

For individual book orders or author interview requests, visit:
GoBackToYourCountry.com
IssaMusharbash.com

To my children,
Sophia, Abraham and Joseph Musharbash

TABLE OF CONTENTS

WHAT PROFESSIONALS ARE SAYING

Despite the increasing potential of technology to share our experiences with one another, as individuals Americans seem increasingly ideologically polarized and isolated—seeing only the lived experiences and stories of those who are just like ourselves. *Go Back to Your Country* provides the opportunity to see an American life through another's eyes. The locations and characters may not be familiar, but every reader can empathize with the lasting pain of childhood bullies, the complacency cultivated by an indifferent boss, and the unceasing determination of a loving parent.

Issa Musharbash offers an intimate look at a young life shaped by the complexities of family, culture and country. Yet in the face of these overwhelming forces which would seem to predetermine his life paths, Issa demonstrates there are always alternatives. His story shows the importance of resilience, and the way this resilience is cultivated by both faith in oneself and meaningful connections with others. Issa's simple narrative style feels like reminiscing with an old friend who casually offers the benefit of their own wisdom without judgment. Yet Issa is still a young man--I look forward to seeing what he does next and I'm proud to call him a friend!

Jerusha Achterberg, MA, MPH
Continuing Education/Special Program Instructor, Division of Continuing Education, Harvard University
Module Director, Office for External Education, Harvard Medical School

Go Back to Your Country! is an awe-inspiring book by an immigrant author. As Issa describes his family's difficult journey to the U.S followed by his challenging teenage life, you can't help but feel what he felt. He uplifts and inspires the reader by overcoming the lowest points of his life. He finds love in his life and success in business. I hope that others who encounter challenges in life will be encouraged by the uplifting message of this book. It is truly an only-in-America story!

James Davis
Mayor, City of Bayonne, NJ

As a Chaplain to the New York Yankees and others in the sports arena, I can smell a spirit of winning from miles away. *Go Back to your Country* is a captivating and promising immigration story that showcases the power of building a dream against all odds. This is the immigration story of the 21st century!

Willie Alfonso
Chaplain, New York Yankees and Brooklyn Nets

Giants can be defeated by underdogs. Around 1020 BC a famous battle took place approximately 90 miles away from Amman, Jordan, the birthplace of the author. It was a battle known for the victory of a young underdog named David who overcame a giant named Goliath. Goliath represents the obstacles, rejection, limitations, intimidation, stereotypes, biases, prejudice, and discrimination that many immigrants like myself face. In *Go Back to your Country* Issa Musharbash shares his compelling and inspirational story as a young immigrant who overcame the odds of achieving success and bears witness to the truth—underdogs can succeed and overcome giants.

Paula Rodriguez
Co-Founder & Lead Pastor, The Cityline Church

Go Back to your Country is a true story of an immigrant boy defying all odds against him and becoming an American entrepreneur. The book is not only filled with tremendous tales of determination and persistence in the grave of hardships, you'll find revealing truths on leadership development. Today, I serve as the CFO of a Real Estate Brokerage that this "immigrant boy" founded and can attest to his true mark of extraordinary leadership. It is my hope that as you read through the pages of this book, you uncover the leadership principles woven into Issa's journey. This book is truly a personal and yet practical guide to creating a legacy of greatness.

Giselle Llerena
Chief Financial Officer Provident Legacy Real Estate Services

While our country is divided on issues like immigration, *Go Back to your Country*! becomes a symbol of unity. The author welcomes us into an intimate view of his family's experience coming to America. What a genuinely refreshing read! As an immigrant myself, I personally connected and identified with the struggles, hopes and leaps of fulfilling a dream. The heartfelt narrative brought me closer to another culture and helped me see how similar we are in our shared experiences and humanity as immigrants. *Go Back to your Country* is timely and raises important questions of our times. Foreign or native, you'll need this book in your collection.

Olga Levina
Founder & Artistic Director, Jersey City Theater Center

Go Back to your Country is one of those rare stories that you wish was yours but would not want to actually live through it. This book is much more than an immigrant success story, it's packed with redemption, perseverance, love, and loving oneself. I highly recommend *Go Back to your Country* to anyone who desires inspiration for life's tough battles not from a step-by-step process, but rather from a thrilling and immersive read.

Victor Ng
Founder and Partner, City Standard Data & Clear Skies Title

The. Wow. Factor. Inspiration in its most organic, raw form! Invest the time for you and your team to read *Go Back to your Country* and simply thank the author later. This book mimics powerful professional gasoline! Every leader requires it. My entire team is reading this book.

Dana. B. Cadena | Keller Williams Realty
Certified Real Estate Trainer leading 1,500+ agents

Hardships often prepare ordinary people for an extraordinary destiny. Real life experiences are often more remarkable, full of unpredictable beauty and strange surprises than fictional stories. *Go Back to your Country* is a story of escalating hope in an astonishing immigration journey. This book will certainly inspire many people in the United States and around the world!

Duda Penteado
Co-Founder & Film Director, Unshakeable Productions

Issa just hit the nail on the head with his dynamic and inspirational book *Go Back to your Country*. Do yourself a favor and buy two books, one for yourself and another for the next generation. Having published 1000+ books during my career inside the publishing world, there has not been a book so timely and relevant. This book is an arrow pointed across a divided nation and I truly believe it hit its "Target" this season.

Peter Lopez
Author, Publisher & Speaker

His separation from his mother coupled with seeing how determined she was to get her children back through much peril, I've come to understand where Issa gets his grit and I admire his hustle! Like an open vessel, embracing key advice from his mother & mentors propelled him to the top. And with character like that, he can only continue to soar. *Go Back to your Country* is a book to keep for generations to come.

Francine Mikhail
Executive Editor, EverythingJerseyCity.com

Go Back to your Country is far more than a motivational book! It's a case study on the human potential. In a world of quick fixes, this story demonstrates how true success begins from within and long-lasting success requires relentless commitment and enduring resolve. This book can inspire you to change the trajectory of your life. Pick it up now!

Rev. Cleo Santiago
Clinical Chaplain, Hudson County Department of Corrections

FOREWORD BY CARLOS HERNANDEZ PHD.

What a Man Can Be, He Must Be

The need to survive, to secure food, water and shelter to sustain one's life and by extension that of the family, undoubtedly represents the most basic and essential of human behavior and motivation. Tragically, even in this, the 21st Century, too many struggle with the reality that they cannot guarantee these essentials to themselves or to their families. And this reality drives or motivates day to day behavior. Such has been the case since the dawn of time and may indeed persist throughout our existence as a species. In recent human history however, there has been a growing trend of humans securing these basic necessities and as a result, motivation pushes away from basic physiological existence to something more ethereal, subjective, or humanistic.

The modern understanding of human motivation was perhaps best captured by psychologist Abraham Maslow who in a groundbreaking 1943 paper entitled *A Theory of Human Motivation*, described the movement from simple survival, to the motivation for social belonging, to the drive for self-esteem and ultimately to the pinnacle of motivation, the drive to self-actualization. Later in his book *Motivation and Personality*, he refined the concept of self-actualization to describe the need to transcend; "to give of oneself to something beyond oneself."

I believe the personal and social dynamic of immigration can be seen from the perspective as the desire of an individual, a family, or even an entire community of people motivated purely by the desire to actualize themselves and even transcend. And indeed within the context of American history self-actualization or transcendence is embodied in the concept of the "American Dream."

Go Back to Your Country presents an insightful, poignant, and contemporary expression of a mother's, a young son's, and a family's desire to flee conditions that were intolerable in their native Jordan and boldly strike out at great peril, to the United States of America to realize their dream of a better life. Beginning with Issa's mother's desire to flee with her family, not knowing whether they would survive or not, to Issa's eventual success as an entrepreneur, the reader travels through a living example of the stages of Maslow's "needs hierarchy." From physiological survival, to the quest for social belonging, to the need for self-esteem, in Issa's story one experiences a palpable sense of the difficulties, trials and triumphs of his journey. In his own words one lives his life's experiences as well as the lessons learned. He has an uncanny ability to draw the reader into his life and feel what he felt as he was buffeted by what was thrown at him and by the honest descriptions of his responses to people and places that impacted him. The chapters reveal the evolution of a young immigrant boy who despite the challenges, bigotry and even violence visited upon him, he emerges whole, healthy, and eager to reshape the world around him. And finally, in his success and desire to help others achieve their own dreams, Issa has achieved, I believe, the transcendence that Maslow described as the pinnacle of human motivation. This book is both a warm and humble, immigration saga as well as a primer on a family's and an individuals journey to discover all that one can be.

This book is as aspirational as it is inspirational. In reading it, one comes away with a sense of optimism and reverence for the human spirit. One celebrates the commitment and perseverance of the immigrant spirit. And one emerges with renewed belief that the story of the immigrant over the centuries is as alive and well today as ever and that we can all learn valuable lessons from uncovering his or her story.

Carlos Hernandez, PhD.
President Emeritus, New Jersey City University

INTRODUCTION BY REV. DR. JOSHUA RODRIGUEZ

As I reflect on my mentorship relationship with the author, Issa Musharbash, I think of precious stones. I truly believe that people are like precious stones that need to be processed in order to discover their unlimited potential and value. The mentorship process can be closely related to the precious stones industry. Over the last 35 years, I have had the privilege of mentoring many men and women with untapped potential and value. In my role, I help them identify their gifts, talents and abilities and then point them in the right direction. I attempt to add value to their lives by providing sincere feedback, guidance, motivation, and emotional support.

A precious stone is a piece of mineral crystal that when cut and polished is used to make jewelry and other ornaments. Precious stones are rare and unique. Science informs us that there are at least five things that are necessary in order to form precious stones. The formation of precious stones requires (1) the necessary ingredients, (2) the right temperature, (3) the correct amount of pressure, (4) the necessary time and (5) space. All of these components can be found in the character and leadership formation of Issa Musharbash. In other words, the author's ethnic background and physical features represents the necessary ingredients. The environment he grew up in, as you see unfold in the following pages represent the right temperature. The rejections, pain, setbacks and failures represent the correct amount of pressure. The length of his journey represents the necessary time and of course, his perceived loneliness represents the necessary space. This combination formed his life and character as a precious stone. If I could put Issa's compelling journey into a few headlines, they would be the following: Breaking Limits. Never Giving Up. Rejecting Rejection. Attaining Breakthrough Results. Refuse to Allow People to Label You. A Diamond in the Rough. Fulfilling your Dreams.

In *Go Back to Your Country* Issa shares his authentic and inspirational story as a young immigrant boy who arrived in America and faced the common challenges that keep most immigrants limited and stagnated; however, he shares how he was able to transcend the obstacles of rejection, racism and discrimination. He decided to work hard and surpass the limitations that many unjust systems and structures place on immigrants.

Just like precious diamonds have different types of cuts, we as humans can experience painful cuts that can ultimately lead to our beauty. Although life appears to send us sharp cuts to hurt us, instead these cuts can actually shape us, if we let them. I have personally had the privilege of being part of Issa's life as a mentor for the last 18 years. I have witnessed the process of cuts that led to Issa's success. I have seen him look at the obstacles and say, "I refuse to let you bring me down—this is my country too and I am going to see my dreams come true!" I have witnessed his persistence and perseverance as an immigrant in learning how to reject rejection. I have also witnessed firsthand his transition from the dangerous life in the streets as a gang banger to becoming a productive member of society and gaining employment at Dunkin' Donuts. I have been honored and fortunate enough to stand on the sidelines and cheer him on in his career from retail to banking and then to real estate, breaking barrier after barrier in unprecedented ways. I have stood proudly by his side as he wed his best friend Ketty, and began to raise a precious family. I have rejoiced with the birth of his amazing children, Sophia, Abraham and my Godson Joseph. I have also been inspired as his mentor to see him give birth to Provident Legacy Real Estate Services. His leadership development has been extraordinary and his ability to dream and create a practical roadmap to achieve those dreams has been so motivating.

If you're looking for "golden nuggets" or precious stones, you'll find them in this book. I highly recommend this book to anyone, regardless of their occupation or legal status. It will encourage you to look at your obstacles as stepping-stones to success and to continue to dream. It will inspire you to overcome adversity and utilize the opposition as an instrument that will put you on the track of success! As Vice-President of the National Latino Evangelical Coalition and advocate for immigrants, I encourage you to read and dream big. Why go back to your country, when you can stay and overcome every imaginable obstacle. Don't go back to your country, instead, stay and defy all odds!

Rev. Dr. Joshua Rodriguez M.Div D.Min
Bishop, The Cityline Church

CHAPTER 1

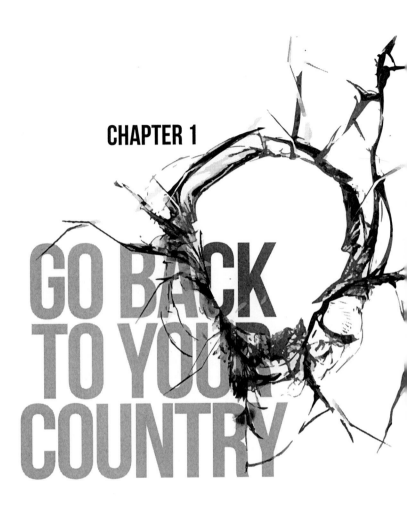

GO BACK TO YOUR COUNTRY

8 years old

"Hey! Hey! What are you doing?"

The older man, Jorge, thumped the boy on the back of his head with his ring finger. "That's not the way you do it!"

The boy winced and grabbed the spot where Jorge's heavy ring had left its mark.

That hurts like heck!

But Jorge didn't seem to care. Instead, he picked up the tray of sodas and turned it around on the table so the labels on the bottles were facing the customers.

"How many times do I have to tell you?" he snarled. "Put the bottles so the customers can read the #*%&! labels!"

The boy stood there for a minute, rubbing his head where his boss had hit him. He didn't know which was worse, the embarrassment he felt at being put down in front of everyone, or the pain on the back of his head.

Jorge was always hitting him on the back of his head with that heavy ring—whenever he did something Jorge didn't like, and sometimes for no reason at all. The ring was a weapon. In the eyes of the boy, it was worn to inflict pain.

The boy was 12 years old, really too young to have a full-time job, but he needed it. His family of six lived in a small attic apartment and he wanted to do whatever he could to help. Lately, that meant enduring a barrage of anger and criticism from his boss. He wouldn't have put up with it, but his family counted on him and they couldn't afford him losing the job. As far as he could remember, this was the first time the boss had ever said a word about turning the soda bottles so the customers could read the labels.

Jorge gave his sweetest smile to the man and woman who had ordered the sodas. "Enjoy!" he said. "Your sandwiches will be right out." When he turned around to face his young employee, the smile quickly transformed into an angry glare.

"Got a delivery for you," he said. "And I want you to make it snappy. No loafing around like you usually do."

The boy turned and went to the counter to pick up the delivery. His head still stung as he muttered under his breath.

"What did you say?" the boss challenged.

"Nothing."

"You want to keep this job? You keep your mouth shut and do what I tell you to do. Now get out of here with that delivery. And hurry!"

The truth was that the boy worked very hard cleaning tables, mopping floors, scrubbing the grill (which was his favorite task) and whatever else was needed including dumping the 5-gallon bucket of waste collected from the grill's grease tray. Every afternoon, as soon as school was out, he took a half-hour bus ride to the sandwich shop, started working at about 3:30 p.m. until at least 9:00 p.m., he took the bus home from Jersey City to Bayonne, and finally got to bed around 11:00 p.m. The next day, he'd get up just in time to get dressed, get to school by 8:40 a.m., and do it all again. He also worked all day on Saturday and Sunday. His record-breaking week consisted of 83 hours, which earned him $269.75.

The boy wanted to say, "I do everything I can to please you, but nothing works. And your standards are constantly changing." He thought better of it, grabbed the order for delivery and headed out toward Newark Avenue.

Despite the anger he was feeling, he felt himself swell with pride as he walked past the Post Office and saw the Stars and Stripes flying high in the sky.

He had spent most of his life in the country of Jordan, but was proud and happy to be a new resident of the land of his dreams, the United States of America.

It was a cold, gray day and he shivered as he walked alone. He wished he'd brought a jacket and was glad he didn't have far to go.

Ah, there was his destination, just ahead on the right. He went in, made the delivery, pocketed the forty dollars and was told to keep the change. Then he headed back up the street toward Kennedy Boulevard. He didn't want to give his boss any reason to say he'd been loafing.

Suddenly, out of nowhere, he heard a swoosh of air behind him, followed by a tremendous blow on the back of his neck. Things went black for just a moment and he tumbled to the sidewalk.

As he tried to struggle to his feet, he saw a group of three or four boys lined up on the sidewalk about 10 or 15 feet in front of him. The biggest, tallest boy, who appeared to be the leader, was wearing a mask like the one Jason wore in the movie, *Friday the 13th*.

Apparently, they had clotheslined him from behind as they ran past. Now they were coming back to finish him off. The older boy stiffened his right arm, held it out in front of himself and aimed it at the boy. He shouted something derogatory—the boy couldn't make it out—and they all charged in his direction.

He wasn't about to let them take that money, so he turned and ran toward Kennedy Boulevard. If he got there, maybe his boss would see him coming, call the police and he'd live to fight another day.

He didn't make it. The biggest of his assailants slammed into him just before he reached the corner, knocking the air out of him and again sending him sprawling to the sidewalk.

"Oh!" he yelled out in spite of himself when one of the boys kicked him in the nose, sending a torrent of blood spraying into the air. He tried to struggle to his feet, but the big guy punched him in the stomach. There was no way he could fight back. He was completely outnumbered.

Still, he wasn't going to let them get that money. He wasn't about to give his boss another reason to be disappointed in him. The boys kept punching and kicking him all over—in the face, the legs, stomach and between his legs.

He was sure they were going to keep on until they killed him. Then, finally, as he was about to crumble into unconsciousness, they stopped.

The big guy knelt down, put his face next to the boy's ear and shouted, "Go back to your #*%&! country". Then they turned and ran, leaving him lying bloody and bruised on the sidewalk. They didn't even try to take the money. This wasn't a robbery. It was a brutal attack, just because he was "a foreigner."

After several minutes on the ground, he got to his feet and limped the rest of the way to the sandwich shop. When he staggered through the door, his boss saw the blood spattered all over him, and came running over to help.

"I have your money," the boy said, with a bloody smile.

"Money?" he said. "Who did this to you?"

He ran to the phone and called the police, and an ambulance.

The next thing the boy knew, he was in the hospital and police were showing him pictures of possible suspects, but he didn't recognize anyone because all he remembered was the mask.

Whomever it was, he secretly wished they would have wanted the money. He thought it would have been better if they were just trying to rob him, rather than beating him up just because he was different. For weeks afterward, he kept hearing those words as he daydreamed: "Go back to your #*%&! country!"

Although they didn't break his bones, they seemingly shattered his long awaited hope.

Welcome to the country he had dreamed of and longed for all of his life…

Welcome to America!

How do I know so much about what happened that awful afternoon?

Simple. I was that boy, and my name is Issa.

America, Land of Opportunity

Some people will tell you that America has lost much of its luster over the past few decades. They say that the United States is no longer the land of opportunity, welcoming immigrants with open arms and providing them with an opportunity to make their dreams come true. Have we really forgotten the contributions made by immigrants? I'm talking about people like Albert Einstein, who was born in Germany; inventor Nikola Tesla, who came to the United States from Croatia; and Eric Ly, co-founder of LinkedIn, who hails from Vietnam. Other prominent immigrants include Anousheh Ansari, the female astronaut born in Iran; Oscar-winning actress Natalie Portman, from Israel; Sergey Brin from Russia who co-founded Google, and the list is endless.

In fact, a study conducted by New American Economy, a bipartisan pro-immigration group, reveals that 45 percent of Fortune 500 companies are founded by immigrants and their children, generating $6.1 trillion in revenue in 2018 alone.

I love seeing the Statue of Liberty standing majestically in the New York Harbor. I am comforted when I see the torch she raises into the sky, and remember the inscription that begins, "Give me your tired, your poor, your huddled masses yearning to breathe free." I believe that the United States is still a land of opportunity and hope in spite of her imperfections.

There have always been people who hated anyone who had a different skin color, wore unusual clothes or had unfamiliar customs. Xenophobia is nothing new. It just breaks my heart to see that it is still alive and well in the United States today. I hear so many inhumane and indecent comments about immigrants, most of whom are good people who have come here to build better lives for themselves and their families. Today's anti-immigrant climate has prompted me to put my own story on paper, to share some of what I have faced after coming to America as a young boy.

Despite the fact that I wasn't always welcomed to America with open arms, this country gave me opportunities that would have been far out of reach in my environment in Jordan. It is only through those opportunities, and the grace of God, that I was able to fulfill some of my greatest dreams of becoming a husband, father and entrepreneur. It was in this nation that I would endure adversity and discover my capacity. I've been granted chances to work my way up with sweat and tears to the top of my profession. While I am not a celebrity entrepreneur with my face splashed over billboards and magazines, I became the CEO of a real estate firm I founded at the age of 26. I envisioned myself empowering associates to also climb to the top and one day take my post as CEO. I accomplished this by the age of 33, gaining a greater degree of freedom than I ever thought was possible.

To be clear, this is not a business or a "how to" book. It's just the story of a 12-year-old boy from Jordan who settled in the U.S.

I'm writing this book for a number of important reasons. First, it's my legacy text, especially for my family, my friends and the many people I've been fortunate enough to know. I hope they find these stories uplifting and inspiring, particularly in times of distress. Second, I hope to inspire you, the reader, to lead a meaningful life. Whether you are an immigrant like me or had the good fortune to be born in the country of your dreams, I have found that a meaningful life is a successful one.

In these stories, I open up my heart to a high degree of vulnerability, sharing tales that have been private for years. I do this with hopes of connecting with you in a meaningful manner. I also hope that you'll pause and reflect during your reading. Perhaps you can find and extract principles that can potentially enable you to overcome challenges that stand between you and your destiny. Native or foreign, I want to remind you that your power is seldomly found at your destination, rather it's built during your journey.

CHAPTER 2

HOW IT ALL BEGAN

Petra, Jordan

"Call an ambulance! Call an ambulance! My baby is burning!"

Lidia was hysterical. Her high-pitched screams seemed to shake the entire house.

Her two-year-old son screamed, too, as she swept him into her arms. "Everything is going to be okay," she whispered, as she wrapped his badly burned body in a warm blanket. It was the middle of winter and cold, with the temperature hovering around -6 Celsius.

The boy was beyond comforting. He screamed even louder as burn blisters began to form on his arms and legs.

The boy's father, Isam, rushed into the kitchen. "What's going on?" he asked. "What happened to him?"

"Hurry and call an ambulance!" his wife shouted. "The pot of boiling tea spilled all over him. We've got to get him to the hospital!"

Without saying a word, Isam ran to the phone and began punching in the number. Within ten minutes, the three of them were on their way to AlBashir Hospital in Amman, Jordan. It only took 30 minutes to get there, but it seemed like hours as the baby continued to cry in pain. By this time, Lidia was sobbing too, while Isam put his arm around her and tried to comfort her.

At the hospital, the family was met by a team of doctors and nurses. The baby was placed on a gurney and wheeled into surgery, while his mom and dad were ushered into the waiting room.

A few minutes later, members of Isam and Lidia's extended family began to arrive. They were upset and a few of them seemed to be angry at Lidia. Instead of offering words of encouragement and hope, they accused her of being an irresponsible mother.

"How could you do this?" one of Isam's sisters-in-law demanded. "How could you burn your baby like this?"

Lidia buried her head in her hands. "I don't know how it happened," she sobbed. "I was watching him. . ."

"Sure, you were." Suggesting otherwise.

A couple of the women exchanged glances, as if Lidia might have tried to hurt her child on purpose. This child brought the mother out of a depression after losing her prior baby at birth. Was she so overwhelmed by the task of caring for her two children that she had tried to kill the youngest one? Such accusations were not uncommon for the young woman, who understandably felt that she had never been completely welcomed into her husband's family.

"I would never hurt my child," she said.

There was no response, except the sound of the wall clock ticking the minutes away. The family sat together in silence, alone in their misery.

Lidia replayed the terrible scene over and over in her mind. She had been in the kitchen, working on dinner, while the baby chattered happily, anxious to help his mom in any way he could. His older brother, four-year-old Jacob, was also there, looking for something he could do to help, as a large pot of tea began to boil on the stove. The tea was safely out of the boys' reach. At least, Lidia thought it was.

Then, suddenly, the unimaginable happened: When Jacob reached for the pot and tried to bring it to the table, the baby, in an attempt to help his brother, accidentally knocked it over. Lidia could only scream and try to grab it, but it was already too late. The whole thing happened so fast! Scalding hot water poured down on the little one, running all over his head and face, and down his body. To make matters even worse, the tea was full of sugar, which caused the cotton knitted sweater to stick to his skin. He had burns on his face, neck, shoulder and other parts of his body.

After what seemed like an eternity, a nurse came into the waiting room and reported that, although the child's burns were serious, his life was not believed to be in danger. There was a collective sigh of relief, as if a fresh, cool breeze had swept into the room. The nurse explained that the doctor would come to see the family as quickly as possible, and give a further update on the boy's condition.

When the doctor finally came, about 20 minutes later, he explained that things were not quite as rosy as the nurse had made them sound. The baby was facing a long, difficult road to recovery. After receiving his uncle's donated blood, he needed to spend the next few weeks in the hospital to recover. He was going to have a few scars on his face and neck that would never go away.

Once again, Lidia began to sob as she thought of her child enduring such an ordeal.

A Child and a Mother

It may come as no surprise to you when I tell you that the baby in this story was me.

Lidia is my mom, and although she was a mother of two young boys, she was just 20 years old on the day I burned myself with the boiling tea. A young girl saddled with the responsibilities of motherhood and dealing with relatives who were ready to blame her for anything that went wrong.

I spent the next two weeks in the hospital, and my mother spent most of that time by my side, comforting me and letting me know that she loved me and that I was going to be all right. That wasn't always easy for her because she also had an active four-year-old to care for. In addition, she was pregnant with my brother Hanna, who would be born five months later, and was enduring all the general aches, pains and tiredness that a pregnancy brought with it.

She also recalls one of the first things I said to her after my accident.

"Mommy didn't burn me," I would tell her. "Jacob didn't burn me. Issa burned me, Issa!"

Apparently, I didn't want my mom to feel bad or take the blame for what had happened to me.

Mercifully, my recovery went as well as could possibly be expected. I was soon up and running around, playing with Jacob. My mother continued to provide tender loving care, long after I went home from the hospital. My burns were treated with a skin cream that cost more than 20 percent of our family budget—which was very tight to begin with. It was costly, but it worked.

Eventually, those "permanent" scars on my face disappeared, and today, the only remainder of my accident is a single small scar on my neck and nearly invisible stains on my upper right arm.

The Struggles of a Child Bride

My mother was only 14 years old when she became engaged to my father, whom she had never met, and who was nearly twice her age. While such arranged marriages were common in Jordan 40 years ago, they have pretty much disappeared as Jordan moved into the 21st century.

Yes, Jordan is an Arab country and predominantly Muslim. It is also a modern and progressive country—one of the safest in the Middle East—and has been described as "An oasis of stability in a sea of turmoil." I grew up in Jordan's capital, Amman, which is not so different from urban cities in the United States. Roads are paved. Homes have running water and electricity. Streets are often clogged with traffic. Many live in high-rise apartments and condos. Winters are cold in Amman, with an occasional dusting of snow. In fact, the weather is not that different from northern New Jersey.

If my parents had an opportunity to get to know each other prior to their marriage—or even met before—they might have discovered that they were not well-suited for each other. My mother was ambitious and strong, a person who wanted a better life for herself and her children. My father was laid-back and mellow, more willing to take life as it came. I always wondered if anyone noticed the lack of compatibility during the marriage negotiations.

My mother was one of 14 children. As you can imagine, with that many children, her family always struggled to get by. As a result of her upbringing, my mother learned how to make the most of very little. My dad earned around 100 dinars (approximately $130 USD) per month, which is not a lot of money, but somehow my mother worked with that tight budget and our house always looked like a palace inside. We always ate well, and my siblings and I were dressed pretty well. Looking back, I still don't know how she did it. She was relentless in her approach to managing tight budgets. She had vision.

Her family fled Armenia during the Armenian Genocide and eventually settled in the city of Aqaba, Jordan's only seaport. They strongly believe that they were the first Christian family to settle in modern day Aqaba. Aqaba sits by the Red Sea, at the southern tip of Jordan and is a warm, sunny place.

My grandmother, Helena, was the role model for the entire neighborhood where they lived. If anyone had a problem of any kind, they would bring it to her, and ask her to help. She tended to sick babies, helped people put their marriages back together, and dispensed motherly advice of all sorts. I vividly recall her deep admiration for King Hussein bin Talal.

King Hussein was known to be a very humble and accessible man, a rarity in a part of the world filled with many ruthless dictators. The king had to survive several assassination attempts carried out by Islamic extremist groups, even though most of the "common people" I knew adored him. Many of these came after Jordan signed a historic peace treaty with Israel in 1994.

I don't remember meeting my maternal grandfather — he passed away before I turned three —but I remember his house. It consisted of five small rooms. My grandmother and her family filled it with joy and lived life to the fullest.

The house was right on the Gulf of Aqaba. It was a short walk—or run, usually—across a sandy beach to the warm, inviting waters of the Red Sea—the same stretch of ocean Moses led the Israelites across as they escaped from Egypt, some 3,500 years ago.

It was in the Red Sea that my mother taught me how to swim, patiently working with me and helping me overcome my fear of putting my head beneath the water.

Extraordinary Mother

You see, my mother was only a young girl, and my father already a grown man. But in many ways, it seemed that my mother was the more mentally and emotionally fit of the two.

My mother was something extraordinary, making sure my siblings and I toed the line and were well-mannered in every situation—whereas my dad was a kind man who never lifted a finger to me or my siblings, or said a critical word to us. My mother was the one who made sure we sat up straight at the table, were respectful to our elders, and administered a sharp slap across the face if she thought we were being rude or disrespectful. Needless to say, I also got smacked if I chewed with my mouth open, scraped the bottom of my plate with my spoon, or committed any one of many other violations. As strange as it may sound, my mother's demands upon me and my siblings translated as pure love. We all knew she disciplined us because she loved us. Her smacks on the cheek may have hurt a little bit, but I am certain that they pained her more. She had an urgency to raise respectful children, and her relentless discipline served as medicine for the soul.

She had also grown up with a very deep faith in God. She told me that when she was a little girl walking to school, she always felt that Jesus was walking alongside her. She spoke to Him as if He was there, holding her hand. My mother went through ceaseless difficulties in her life, but somehow was able to endure the heat of it long enough.

As a young girl, going to school was my mother's biggest dream. Most women were highly discouraged from going. She ultimately wanted to be a fashion designer. In the 1970s and 80s, her family still did not see the value of education for women. They felt that the need for women to serve at home outweighed their education. It was important for young girls to learn how to cook full meals, prepare and serve coffee and tea to visitors, and keep a house in tip-top shape.

My uncles allowed my mother to go to school as long as she paid for it. Fortunately, she got an after school job helping the nuns. They would sweep the debris off the entire school yard with large brooms and mop all the hallways and classrooms at the end of the day. She enjoyed working after school because that time provided her with more of an opportunity to talk to God, and that, in turn, made the time pass by quickly. Regrettably, that education couldn't continue; it came to a halt at the age of fourteen, right before her objectionable wedding day.

Opposites Don't Always Attract

Now, my mom was a beautiful girl, who at the age of 14 had the face and figure of a 21-year-old. She was slender and curvy with large luminous eyes, long dark hair and a dazzling smile. Men gazed at her everywhere she went, which was one reason why her parents and older siblings were anxious to get her engaged and married. Her beauty caused them to fear for her safety. What if someone kidnapped and raped her? At the very least, she and the family would be completely disgraced. At worst, she could be seriously injured or killed.

As for my dad, his parents wanted him to get married because it was the right time. His older brother had recently married, thus expediting his turn. Like many Middle Eastern families, they expected their four boys to get married in chronological order, from the oldest to the youngest. However, the difficulty was that he didn't have a steady job. In fact, at the age of 25, he didn't have financial stability as his older brother did. Instead, at the direction of his parents he stayed home and took care of household tasks. He was a plumber who kept the families' estate in good working order. He kept the home clean, changed curtains and handled other household chores.

Unlike my mom's family, the Musharbash clan was well-known in Jordan. Since the establishment of the kingdom, members of the family held positions in military and politics. They are recognized today for their influence in the business sector, particularly in finance and real estate. My grandfather had been a cook in the Jordanian army and did pretty well for himself, although he wasn't nearly as prosperous as the rest of his family.

My dad grew up in a beautiful and spacious two-story house in an elegant part of the Jordan's capital city, Amman. My grandfather owned the prime property, which included three commercial stores that he leased to merchants and two apartments he rented to faithful tenants. The income it produced took care of the family's needs.

My parents did their best to make their marriage work, and when I was a little boy, I never knew there was any difficulty or frustration between them, but they were too different in too many important ways.

A World Beyond

I was a very young boy when my eyes were opened to the possibility of a greater world "out there" far beyond the borders of Jordan. I recall my father obtaining a job with British Airways', though it didn't pay all that much. He wasn't an executive, but he dressed like one, and he often joked that he was the pilot.

Although my dad didn't travel himself, his job brought British Airways catalogues and magazines into our home. I mentioned earlier that my siblings and I always dressed very well. My mom credits this opportunity as she was able to order clothes through the British Airways catalogue and receive an employee discount.

I remember feeling amazed that so many of the clothes I wore came from a far-off place called Great Britain. It must be an amazing place indeed to create beautiful clothes like these! I wanted to know more about it, and all the beautiful places I saw through the photographs in British Airways' magazine.

Somehow, I knew, even then, that I would find my destiny out there, somewhere beyond the borders of the Middle East.

CHAPTER 3

TASTE OF OPPORTUNITY

Issa, Hanna, Jacob

"Issa, we're going to America!"

I had never seen such a huge smile on my mother's face.

I wasn't really sure what or where America was, but if my mom was excited, then I was excited, too!

Over the last several weeks, my older brother and I had heard our mom and dad whispering about America. Apparently, some of our relatives lived there, and we knew from the way our parents talked that it must be a magical land—like Great Britain, perhaps. As usual, my mother was more excited than my dad was, but even he seemed uncharacteristically animated and full of energy.

I didn't know it at the time, but my mom and dad had traveled to the United States once before, spending several months with relatives in California while my mother was pregnant with me. I came within days of being born in California, which would have made me a natural born American citizen. Instead, we returned to Jordan just before my birth.

I think my mother had always had her eyes on the United States. As my baby brother Hanna was born, his arrival had reignited my mother's desire to see her children grow up in America. She felt that my siblings and I were entrusted to her by God, and she knew that in the United States, we could get an excellent education and go on to make something out of ourselves.

The Promised Land

It was a long time ago, but I still remember how my heart pounded with excitement as we boarded that airliner and headed off to a brand-new life. We were leaving everything we had ever known, but my mind was focused on the future rather than the past.

This time my family would stay in the United States for about three years, most of it with an aunt and uncle in Jersey City, New Jersey—but there was very little evidence that my mother's hopes for our life in America would come true. My dad had trouble finding a steady job. It's no wonder, really, because he was in his mid-30s and didn't speak more than a few words of English. Neither did my mother, who took care of three boys while carrying another baby on the way. He took on a succession of low-level jobs that usually lasted for a month or two, and then he found himself unemployed again. As a result of my dad's job troubles, we moved from one small apartment to another, and finally wound up living with my aunt and uncle and their three children, which wasn't easy for a number of reasons. There were a large number of us jammed into that little apartment with only one bathroom. There were two fathers striving to be the heads of their family, and two women (who loved cooking) with only one kitchen, stove and refrigerator. We couldn't help but step on each other's toes.

My mother would take my siblings and I out to parks, to enjoy the open spaces and get a chance to run around and exercise our muscles. I know my mother must have dreaded taking us back to that little apartment at the end of the day, and to be honest, I'm pretty sure my aunt and uncle dreaded it, too. We loved each other, but we had learned that there is such a thing as too much togetherness.

As for the parks, they were green and pretty, but they weren't all that safe.

Hanna, who was just a toddler, was run over by a man on a bicycle and spent a couple of days in the hospital. Shortly after that, Jacob fell out of a swing and broke his arm. Sometimes it seemed like it was one catastrophe after another.

"Do you boys know where you're going?"

One day, my mother ran out to her prenatal appointment, and left me and my younger brother Hanna at home in my father's care. He had been out all day looking for a job and was exhausted. Despite his efforts to stay awake, he quickly nodded off. I was about four years old at the time, and Hanna was two, and what seemed like an adventure, we decided to take a walking tour of Jersey City.

We headed out the door, and made our way to Kennedy Boulevard, which is one of the busiest streets in the city. Cars whizzed past us as we walked past stores of all kinds: barber shops, dollar stores, pharmacies, department stores and more. If I had given it any thought, I would have realized that we were hopelessly lost and would never be able to find our way home. I was too engrossed in our adventure to think about that.

Then suddenly I heard a voice ask, "Do you boys know where you're going?"

I looked up into the concerned face of a Jersey City police officer. At first, I thought he was a giant!

Thankfully, I had been going to kindergarten, where I had gained a pretty good grasp of the English language.

I took a couple of steps backwards and looked up and down the street. For the first time, I realized that I didn't have a clue where we were.

Thinking fast, I gave my best answer:

"Nowhere."

The officer's mouth turned up at the corners as he tried to stifle a smile.

He stooped down to our level and asked, "Do you know where your mom is? Is she nearby?"

I shook my head, and Hanna whimpered as he looked around for her.

The police officer asked us if we knew where we lived.

As a matter of fact, I did! Even though I had no idea where it was, I had memorized the address for a kindergarten assignment, and gave it to the officer.

"Well, come on boys," he said, waving us in the direction of his patrol car, "I'll take you home."

What a thrill it was to ride in the back of that beautiful black and white car, with all the lights, buttons and amazing gadgets. Our excitement disappeared when we pulled up in front of our apartment and saw that my mother was just arriving home at the same time. For the first time, it occurred to me that we were in trouble. The policeman started in on her.

"Where have you been? How could you go off and leave your children alone to wander off like this? You could be in big trouble for child neglect and could even go to jail." The officer went on to call DYFS, formerly known as the New Jersey Division of Youth and Family Services.

Mom didn't know much English, but she had learned enough to understand some of what he was saying, and she knew it wasn't good. Her face turned crimson, and she sputtered, "But…I left them with my husband. He was supposed to be watching them."

The officer banged on the door, and my dad arrived, still wiping the sleep from his eyes. Becoming aware of what had transpired, he apologized profusely. He hadn't meant to fall asleep, but he was just so tired! The officer canceled the DYFS complaint when he saw that my dad was, in fact, home.

My mother was furious, of course, and it took some time before the incident was forgotten.

Unfortunately, things did not get better after that. No opportunity came to my dad to make himself a hero and thereby win back my mother's admiration and respect. He didn't get a high-paying job so we could get our own place to live—a place with our own bathroom, or maybe even two. My siblings and I did not suddenly become the world's best-behaved children.

In the midst of these circumstances, my expecting mother longed for a baby girl. After giving birth to three boys, she was hoping she would finally have a baby girl. And just as she wished, in November of 1990 she gave birth to Mariana, who gave her a new joy and sense of hope. Mariana was the first of my siblings to be born in America.

Return to Jordan

A bit reluctantly, my parents finally decided that our effort to begin a new life in America had fallen short of the goal. We would go back to Jordan, move in with my dad's parents and start building a life there again. Although I was only a child, I could sense my mother's disappointment. She had liked living in the United States and so had I.

I was still a small boy, and we had been in the States long enough that many of my memories from Jordan had started to fade. I didn't feel like I was going "home," because Jordan was no longer familiar to me. But of course, wherever my mother and father went was home to me, and I was happy just to be with them.

My dad went home first, and I didn't ask why. I guess I assumed he was going to make preparations for our arrival. If I had thought about it, I might have realized that it was a sign that all was not well between my parents. In the midst of it all, my mother never made any remarks to make us feel like their marriage was in trouble. She never spoke ill of dad, even to this day, and that kept our relationship with him healthy.

Now it was time for the rest of us to go back to Jordan. For financial reasons, we couldn't take a direct flight to Amman from JFK. We had to stop in Cairo for a few days to catch a connecting flight.

During our time in the United States, we had established a good friendship with a business man named Gamal Salama. He owned the grocery store near our apartment on Central Ave in Jersey City. Gamal had immigrated to the US from Egypt at a young age and became a US Citizen. Consequently, when we found out about the stop in Cairo, we called Gamal. Thanks to Gamal, we did not spend those few days at Cairo International Airport. He connected us with his brother in Cairo, who put us up for a few days until our time to take the flight to Amman. Gamal's brother and his family graciously took us in and treated us with much kindness. It was something we always remembered with gratitude.

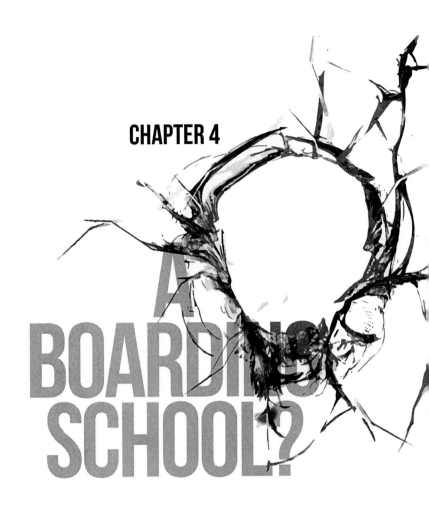

CHAPTER 4

A BOARDING SCHOOL?

THEODOR SCHNELLER SCHOOL
Founded In
Jerusalem 1860 - Amman 1959

Away From Home

I couldn't believe what I was hearing.

We had been back in Jordan for only a few weeks. Barely long enough to get reacquainted with my grandfather and grandmother in Amman.

My mother was telling me that my little brother and I were going away to attend school at the Theodor Schneller School for Orphans and Marginalized Children. I didn't know much about the school, except that it was a school for boys founded by Christian missionaries from Germany—and, as the name implied, most of the kids who went there were desperately poor.

I wanted to protest that we were not orphans, nor were we poor. At least we didn't seem poor. But my mother explained that my grandparents had some contacts there, and they had managed to get us in.

"Do you understand, Issa?" my mother asked.

"Yes," I answered, trying to be brave for her sake. "But what about Jacob?"

"I've already explained that to you," she answered. "Jacob will stay and go to school here. Only you and Hanna were accepted in this school; they did not have room for Jacob."

"But…will you come and see me?"

"As often as I possibly can."

I didn't think it was fair that Jacob would get to stay at home while Hanna and I were sent away. I admit to being envious of Jacob, feeling that he was obviously my parents' favorite child, the first born—but as far as I recall, I never let on. I wanted to be a good boy, to do whatever my mother and father wanted and needed me to do. For now, that meant enrolling in the Theodor Schneller School, which was located in the city of Russeifa, about 12 miles northeast of Amman. Russeifa is a city in Zarqa Governorate in Jordan and part of the Amman metropolitan area, which now has a total population of well over 4 million.

It was not until I became an adult that I learned of my paternal grandparents' reasons to send us away to boarding school. One good. One not so good.

My grandparents believed they were looking out for us, apparently making this a "good decision". We had spent nearly three years in the United States and had picked up "American" ways. Hanna and I had learned a great deal of English. In fact, we both spoke English much better than we spoke Arabic. Because of this, we were likely to get singled out and picked on if we went to a rugged Jordanian public school. Another thing that must have fit into the equation was that my grandparents were already providing an apartment to my family, free of charge. Maybe they wanted dad to grow up and take responsibility for his family. Naturally, they were looking for a way to save on other costs, and one of the ways they could do this was to have us attend a school like Schneller, instead of going to an expensive private school in the city of Amman. My parents would have rather had us at home—but what could they do? This way, we would be sure to get a good, Christian education, and it was basically free.

The not-so-good reason was that my parents were not getting along that well. My mother was becoming frustrated with what she saw as my dad's dependence on his parents, and his inability to be the responsible head of his family. We were innocent children oblivious to the realization that my parents were headed for a divorce. As a result, my grandparents wanted to make it highly difficult for my mother to leave the area and take us with her.

Safe, but Away from Home

For the most part, despite my bouts of homesickness, I felt like I was in a good place. Certainly, there were many benefits to life in a boarding school. We got plenty of nutritious (though not necessarily delicious) food to eat. Every student had his own warm, safe bed to sleep in at night. We got free medical care, which was important to me, because I often got a violently bloody nose that required medical attention. Looking back on it, it seems to me that I had one of these episodes every few days—at least once per week—and I could not get the bleeding to stop on my own. The problem wasn't serious, but it persisted for several years, most likely brought on by the dry, hot weather.

True to her word, mom came to see us with our baby sister Mariana as often as she could, but it didn't seem very often to me—or at least it wasn't as often as I wanted it to be. I know now that my parents were dealing with their challenges which made it difficult for either one of them to come see us. Unbeknownst to my brothers and me, their marriage was completely unraveling. When my mother did come to see us, she showed us so much love that we felt it still, even after she had gone back home. We knew she loved us and wanted us home with her. She didn't want us to be all alone so far from home, but there wasn't anything she could do about it.

I was lonely, especially at night, but I accepted that it was the way it had to be.

One thing that made my loneliness painful was that although Hanna and I were at the same school, we were not able to see each other often. Students lived in dormitories that were organized by grade, and Hanna was two years younger than me. We did not have the comfort that might have come from being together, except on weekends. In fact, most of the other boys went home when Friday came, but not my brother and me. We almost always remained. I comforted myself with the thought that I was going to grow up someday and things would be different then. Now, I was only a child and had absolutely no control over what happened to me. But someday, I would control my own destiny. It may seem strange for a young child to take such a long-range view of things, but perhaps I thought that way because I had no choice.

One of the things that caused a lot of anxiety for me and Hanna— besides being separated from our parents—was that we were different from most of our classmates. There were nights I would hear children crying, and I knew these were the ones who had lost one or both of their parents. I missed my mom and dad, too, but at least I had parents to go home to. I also saw, by the way they dressed and the scarcity of their possessions, that many of the children were in desperate need. They had almost nothing, while my brother and I seemed rich by comparison. For these reasons, we found it somewhat hard to fit in.

Things gradually became better for us, and especially for me, when Jacob joined us at the school at the start of our second year. Jacob was assigned to the same building, in the dormitory right next to mine. We didn't mix too much because Jacob's grade slept on one side of the building, and my grade was on the other. Still, I saw him regularly and that was a comfort to me, especially at the end of the day when night was falling.

The school itself sits on 173-acres in the center of the city. There are dormitories, classrooms, and other buildings constructed around one of the largest soccer fields I've ever seen. There are around 70 staff members to care for somewhere between 200 and 300 students. According to the Christian Science Monitor, half of the students are Palestinian refugees, "and most of them from families where poverty, abuse, or neglect endangers their futures—as well as that of others."

The Monitor continues, "The boys live in seven houses with upbeat names such as House of Happiness." Dorm rooms are airy and clean, with a row of beds along one wall and closets on the other. Each house has a mix of first to ninth-graders and a house father who lives there with his family. I lived in the "House of Peace".

"To the newcomers, this is a haven where they find shelter, food, physical safety, and the assurance that tomorrow will bring more of the same. As the year progresses, the walls fill with posters, the bedside tables sprout treasures, and the house becomes home."

The Boy with Long Hair

Still, everything was not peace and love.

Although there were plenty of caring and loving teachers, house parents and administrators at the school, there were some who concentrated on discipline and enforcing the rules, and in a way that terrified me. We were all expected to have neatly trimmed hair—no long hair spilling over our collars or haircuts that departed from "the norm" in any way.

Now, we had to get up at 5 a.m. each morning, get dressed, make our beds, clean, sweep and mop the entire dormitory before heading to the cafeteria. Then we would gather for the Jordanian Pledge of Allegiance and our morning prayer before sitting down to eat breakfast. Everything was very organized and regimented, military-style, which was good because it taught us discipline.

On one of these occasions—right after summer vacation—Mr. Tadros, one of our principals (he was in charge of the dormitories) spotted a boy in the crowd who had come back to school with long hair. This was unacceptable! Mr. Tadros walked over, grabbed the boy's hair and began dragging him across the room.

The boy, who was probably eleven or twelve years old, yelled out in pain and instinctively tried to protect himself. He was no match for the principal, who dragged him by his hair all the way to the front of the cafeteria and gave him a harsh beating for his defiance of school rules. I don't know why the boy didn't get a haircut. Perhaps his parents thought his hair looked fine. Or maybe they were too poor to take him to a barber shop. No matter, the boy's hair did not meet school standards, and, as far as Mr. Tadros was concerned, he had to pay the price publicly.

Strangely enough, Mr. Tadros was kind to me and my brothers. We were afraid of him, as all the students were, but I can't remember him ever really giving us a hard time. I think he knew the situation in our family, and that we were caught in a custody battle between my parents. I'd like to believe he understood what our mom was going through and was sympathetic to her. It seems that when one of his own children was very young, he was diagnosed with a serious illness that could only be treated in America.

Thankfully, his child was cured of his illness after several months of treatment. In the meantime, Mr. Tadros knew what it was like to be separated from his children. Underneath his tough exterior, his heart was not so tough.

CHAPTER 5

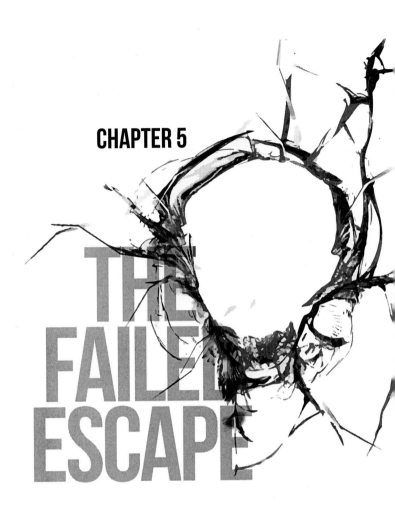

THE
FAILED
ESCAPE

Mariana and the boys

We faced many difficult times at school, but the greatest and most heart wrenching of them all was not being able to see our mother for countless weeks.

What I didn't know was that my parents' marriage was irretrievably broken, and mom was working hard on a plan to get us back to the United States. Apparently, the decision to put us in this school officially put the nail in the coffin of my parents' marriage. I found out later that my mom had felt helpless ever since we were put in the school. She feared that she might lose us forever. Right away, she started working on a plan to get back to America, and then to bring us there to live with her. On several occasions, she went to the American embassy to apply for a visa but was always turned down. Nine, ten times she went, and was always rejected.

Then a friend told her, "Every time they see your passport stamped rejected, they reject you again. So why don't you tear up the passport and say you lost it—or that it was washed in the laundry—something like that?"

So, she tried that. But losing a passport is a big problem in Jordan and carries a substantial fine. Nevertheless, she reported her passport stolen twice, but on the second time she was told, "If you lose your passport again, you're going to jail."

Of course, my mom was devastated, and was crying as she left the building. That's when one of the security guards came up and asked if he could talk to her for a moment. "I've seen you here quite a few times," he said, "and I'd really like to help you. But it's not safe to talk here."

He asked for her phone number and told her that in a couple of days she would get a phone call from a woman named Eunice. Sure enough, the phone call came, and Eunice asked my mother to meet her at an out-of-the-way location so they could talk.

When they met, she told my mother that her associates would be able to provide her with a visa, but that she would have to hand over her passport, which she did. "Eunice" was unclear about how much this would cost.

A couple of weeks later, they met again in the lobby of an airport. As time dragged on, without anything happening, my mom became increasingly frustrated. The situation became worse when she began receiving strange phone calls from men, asking how much she was willing to pay to get the visa. They wanted 11,000 Jordanian dinars, which is roughly the equivalent of 16,000 U.S. dollars. When she said she didn't have that much money, they asked flirtatiously, "Well, how much do you have?" That was the end of it for my mother!

She was determined to get her passport back.

Somehow, she had tracked these people to a run-down building in a very rough and highly dangerous neighborhood. She decided to go there and demand that they give her the passport back and took a brave young girlfriend along with her. To get there they had to travel in and out of backyards, through basements—it was like something out of a spy novel.

Unfortunately, the criminals they were dealing with seemed to know they were coming. When they finally reached their destination, a couple of men stepped out of the shadows and grabbed them. They gagged my mom so she couldn't scream, tied her hands behind her back and locked her in a tiny, dark room. Her friend was locked in another room.

As my mother sat in the darkness, she felt almost certain that the men were going to come back and kill her and that no one would ever find out. All she could do was cry out to God in her mind and ask him to help her. She waited for at least an hour before the men came back. They had her friend with them. Much to her surprise, they untied her, handed over her passport and told her, "Now you and your friend get out of here." She didn't get the visa she was after, but at least she was still alive.

In Egypt

My mother has never been one to give up. Although her plan had failed, she began looking for another way to get us to America.

Surprisingly, uncle Hamparsoum (my mother's older brother) received a call from Gamal Salama. Gamal's brother had died and he wanted to inform my uncle that he had come to Egypt to bury him. How sad! That was the man that put us up while we waited in Egypt for a few days. Uncle Hamparsoum and his wife Iskouhi, who was my mother's best friend and confidant during this season, insisted that my mom go to Egypt and pay her respects to Gamal and his family.

At the time, Gamal was also going through a tough divorce. I think my uncle and aunt's intentions were to set up my mother with Gamal. My uncle convinced my mother to take Mariana and accompany him on this trip. They both told my father's family that mom was joining my uncle on a business trip since his wife can't go. At that point, my uncle took my mother to Egypt and I believe that was the beginning of a new love story. Gamal became my mother's new sign of hope.

It was during her stay in Egypt and with Gamal's help, that my mother came up with another plan to get us to the United States. Gamal purchased a condo in Egypt to provide us with privacy and that affirmed to my mother that he genuinely cared for us. She would take us to Cairo and keep us hidden there until we could arrange transportation to the United States.

So, that's what she did. Although I have no evidence to prove this, I believe that Mr. Tadros helped her get us out of the school.

What a thrilling time it was for me and my brothers when we were told to collect our things and go. We didn't really know where we were going or why, but we knew that we were going to be with our mom, and that was all that really mattered.

We managed to make it safely to Egypt, where we stayed for several weeks, hiding in a rather run-down neighborhood in the ghettos of Cairo. I had seen poverty before, but nothing like this Coptic Christian neighborhood.

Meanwhile, my dad and my grandparents had contacted the authorities and told them that my mother had kidnapped us. Not sure if our names were all over the news, we knew people were looking for us. Our plan was to wait until things settled down and then head to the United States.

Unfortunately, we never made it out of Egypt.

Instead, we were intercepted at the airport by Interpol.

I remember shouts and confusion, being restrained by the police and seeing uniformed officers starting to put handcuffs on my mother. Some of her siblings were there and begged the officers not to arrest her. Thankfully, one of my mom's influential brothers was able to convince them not to put handcuffs on her. Culturally, that was very important because it minimized the potential embarrassment to the family name.

Because of my uncle's influence, she never spent any time in jail. As for Hanna, Jacob and I, it was back to Amman and the Theodor Schneller School for Orphans and Marginalized Children. My mother went back to deal with the erratic demands of my father's family and try to find another way to get us to America.

Making the Most of Things

Although we were not happy to be back at school, it wasn't all bad.

For example, the man who was in charge of the boys in my dormitory— Mr. Issa, actually—was an especially kind and caring man. He was firm with us, but also gentle in his approach. Mr. Issa, who taught Art and English, was fond of me because I shared his name, and spoke English so well. He seemed to be amazed that I had learned "The ABC Song" during my short time in the United States, and often had me stand up and sing it for the rest of the class. I still remember how singing the ABCs in front of my class earned me some much-needed respect among my peers.

Christmas was one of the fondest memories I had needless to say, it's a wonderful season. Every boy received a Christmas gift in the form of a brightly wrapped shoebox full of goodies. Every box was chock-full of things we needed. A toothbrush and toothpaste, warm socks, shampoo, a comb, pencils, notebooks, etc., and there were usually some little toys or a bit of candy. Every year, I was amazed to see how many meaningful items can fit inside a shoebox.

Getting one of those gifts was a highlight of the year, and it wasn't just because of the goodies. The best thing was that those gifts came to us from people overseas who cared about us even though they didn't really know us. Although my parents had separated from each other and from us, these shoeboxes reminded us that we weren't alone, forgotten or abandoned.

We understood, from telephone calls, that mom had married Gamal and gone to America with our little sister Mariana. She promised that she would bring us to be with her as soon as possible, but we did not see her again for another 31 months.

We did not receive many calls from my mother during this time, but we knew she was safe and well in the United States. Although she often told us that she couldn't wait for us to join her in America, my brothers and I wondered why she didn't come to get us. Had she decided that her life was better without us? Those were indeed lonely times. I missed my mother terribly and had just about given up on the thought that I would ever see her again—not dismissing the struggle I had with the idea of having another dad.

On one occasion, we went to spend a weekend with my aunt, who was in touch with my mother, and she put us on the phone with her. My brothers and I all cried and asked her over and over again when she was coming to get us. We knew she was working on it, but she didn't have any answers.

CHAPTER 6

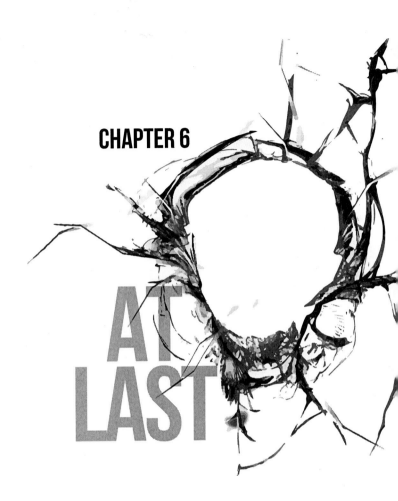

AT
LAST

Schneller 2019 Blackberry Field

One glorious afternoon, I was with a group of my classmates picking blackberries in a field in the middle of our campus. It was a bright, beautiful sunny day, and the berries were so tasty and so full of juice that my friends and I were eating almost as many as we were getting in our baskets.

From my vantage point in the blackberry field, I had a panoramic view of the campus, from the olive trees at one end to the open fields at the other end. As I often did, I was daydreaming about how I would feel on the day my mother would come to get me. I popped a couple of juicy berries in my mouth and smiled as I imagined how she would wrap her arms around me and tell me that she had come to take me away to a better place. I didn't know when that day would happen, but oh, how I hoped it would be soon.

I was just about to take another bite when I suddenly heard someone calling my name. I turned in the direction of the sound and saw a classmate running toward me, his legs churning up a cloud of dust as he sped toward me as fast as he could go.

"Issa! Issa! Your mother's here."

I couldn't hear the last part.

"What?" I shouted at him, cupping my hand behind my ear so I could hear him better.

"Your mother's here!" he shouted again. "She's in the principal's office."

This time I heard him perfectly, and I didn't wait to hear any more. I dropped my basket, spilling blackberries everywhere, and sprinted toward the principal's office.

It was at least a half-mile away, and I'm sure I covered the distance in record time. My heart was pounding with excitement. I couldn't believe that my mother, who had been thousands of miles away for so long, was now so close.

As I ran, a gentle breeze caressed my face, and I felt an exhilarating feeling of liberation wash over me. Free! I was free! My life would never be the same. I was running toward my dreams and into my destiny.

I was moving as fast as my legs could carry me, but it was just like in the movies. The whole thing seemed to be happening in slow motion, and I felt as if I would never actually reach the place where my mother was waiting.

I couldn't contain my emotions as I finally reached the principal's office, ran through the door and saw her standing there, waiting for me, even more beautiful than I remembered her. Tears streamed down my face as did hers as we fell into each other's arms; after 31 long months, to finally embrace each other and go home. I was a young man by this time—a seventh grader—and I knew I was "too big" to cry. But I didn't care what anyone else thought! My mother had come to take us home, and that was all that mattered.

What a joyful day that was! A shocking one, too. In fact, my little brother Hanna was so surprised by my mother's arrival that he couldn't speak. He opened his mouth, but nothing came out.

"Oh, honey," my mother said, "I should have let you know I was coming. I wanted to surprise you, but I didn't want to make you go into shock."

He just stood there with his mouth open. It was several minutes before he was able to tell her how thrilled he was to see her and how much he loved her.

That was my last day in Theodor Schneller School. After our tearful reunion with mom, my brothers and I began making plans for our flight to the United States.

Someone Asked the Right Question

We found out later that ever since my mother had arrived in the United States, she had been trying desperately to bring us there. She didn't really understand the U.S. immigration laws, or have the best grasp of the English language, and she couldn't get anyone to help her. She also could not afford an attorney. Instead, each time she contacted the U.S. Immigration Service, she ran face first into a brick-wall. Whenever she thought she had done everything necessary to bring us to the United States, she was given another hoop to jump through. Sometimes she was provided with translators to help her, but she was never sure if they were translating her words properly. It was a nightmare. She was distressed and upset, missing her boys desperately, but it seemed that no one would go an extra step, much less an extra mile, to try to help her. Furthermore each call cost her a hefty $4.00 per minute.

She called so many times that the people who answered the phone immediately recognized her voice and called her by name. She cried, pleaded and told them how much she missed her children, but the response was always the same. "I'm sorry, but there's nothing more I can do."

My poor mother was also going through a difficult time dealing with some "family members" in Jordan—she never told who they were—who apparently thought she was off having a great time in the United States while her children were suffering in a school for orphans. They would often call her collect and demand to know when she was coming for us.

"You've got to come get your boys," they would say. "They're in terrible shape. They don't have any decent clothes to wear, their shoes are falling apart and they're not getting enough to eat. If you saw them, you'd think they were homeless."

None of this was true. Imagine the added pain in each one of those phone calls.

Then one day, as my mother made yet another phone call to the U.S. Immigration and Naturalization Service, she was connected to one of the world's rarest individuals—a government employee who deeply cared and wanted to help.

Everything changed when she asked my mother a simple question: "How did you get to the United States?"

"Well," my mother answered, "I came with my husband. He's a U.S. citizen, but he's not the father of my children."

There was a shocked silence on the other end of the line. Then the woman asked, "Did you say your husband has United States' citizenship?"

"Yes, that's right."

"And you have custody of your children?"

"Yes."

"Then you don't have anything to worry about. In our eyes, he is their father, and you can have your children within six months."

As strange as it seems, nobody had ever asked her that question before. The fact that she was married to a U.S. citizen changed everything. Therefore, what should have taken six months, took nearly three years.

My mother had reached an agreement with my father and his family. In exchange for full custody of her children, she renounced all claims of child support or alimony from the Musharbash fortune.

Understanding My Father

I love my father and understand him. There was something mysterious about him. When you talk to him, you instantly know that you're talking to a good-hearted fellow. During his time in America, he had purchased this fairly expensive pressure pump designed for unclogging plumbing pipes. You'd have to pump the device to a certain pressure level before shooting out the air to unclog the pipes. In Jordan, most of his competitors were still using the "snake" and making a mess. He kept his work clean, using the pressure pump.

It was a cool-looking thing, all metal and round like a water gun. My siblings and I enjoyed helping my father when it was time to pump the machine. He would finish his work in five to ten minutes but felt bad charging the 50 dinars so quickly. He would ask his clients to boil large pots of water for him, so he could pour them into the area he just pumped out to cleanse any residue. This bought him additional time to justify his fee. He would leave the room he worked in and his machine meticulously clean before leaving. At the end of his job, you would see his smile burst through all the sweat in his face, and the satisfaction of a job well done beamed through his eyes.

It still took me years to figure him out and get a better grip on his actions and inactions. I've asked myself many times, "Why did he not defend my mother against the demands of his parents as any good husband would?" "Why did he agree to put us in a boarding school?" These questions lingered in my mind for most of my teenage years. "Why this and why that?"

My mother always defended him and protected his reputation in front of us children. As I got older, I pressed my mother for answers and she finally explained.

"Issa, your dad is a good man. He is just a little naive and it's not totally his fault."

"What do you mean?"

"You see, when he was a young boy, his mother relied on him to help around the house. Rather than going outside with his siblings and playing with them, he stayed at home. He learned how to sew curtains, sheets, and anything that his mother needed. I guess, unintentionally, instead of turning into a man, he turned into a maid."

"Tell me more"

"Now, his brothers went outside the house and developed as most boys do. He never had the chance to develop that way. He was an innocent and obedient boy, tending to all of his mother's cares."

"Go on."

"This crippled him, Issa. This must have been a critical factor in his childhood development. I defended him, publicly and privately. I made sure no one would speak ill of him. If someone dared, I gave them a piece of my mind."

As tears dripped down her face, I leaned in and said "I understand, Mom. I understand"

"I was willing to carry this burden for the rest of my life as long as you and your siblings had opportunities. I can endure hardships and mistreatments, but I just couldn't endure it happening to my children."

There is much more to this story—but that's when I began to understand my father. My "daddy issues" did not suddenly disappear, but I was able to navigate through them, or at least I thought so at this point. It would be the last time I saw my father in fourteen years.

CHAPTER 7

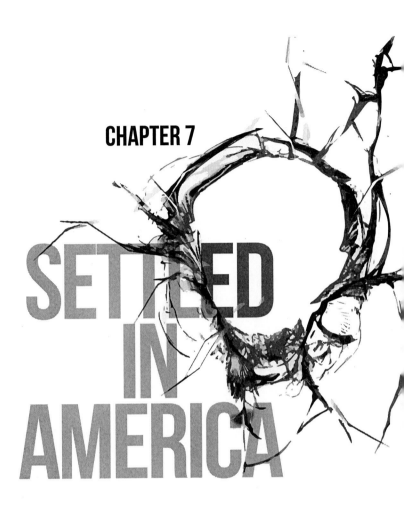

SETTLED
IN
AMERICA

Baby Melad

To say that I was thrilled to be going back to the United States is an understatement. I had so many pleasant memories from my earlier days here, and figured I'd just pick up where I left off—but things were very different now. First, I was not in a rush to embrace my "new dad". I thought that every brick I'd use to build a relationship with my step dad would cost me a brick from my relationship with my biological dad. At some point, I would end up with two half-built relationships.

We were now part of a blended family with eight children. We were fortunate to get along very well, but more so, we were all thrilled when my mother eventually gave birth again. Our baby brother, Melad, brought us together in a profound way. After his birth, there was no denying that we were all members of one family: a family who cared and loved each other. We always joked that Melad was the glue that bonded us together. His dad (my stepfather) had four children from his first marriage, and his mom (also my mom) had four children from her first marriage. Melad was the bridge.

As I shared earlier, things were not the same in the U.S. The sweetness and light of the kindergarten years had been replaced by the anger and cruelty of grammer school, and I was a frequent target, simply because I was different.

I was naïve to assume I would be welcomed; I didn't know I was "so" different. The boys at my school in Jordan never seemed to think there was anything odd about me—well, maybe a little—but it didn't take long for my classmates in America to ensure that I felt out of place. It happened on the very first day, the first time I went to the lavatory.

"Hey, kid, where'd you get that nose?"

A boy about my size was staring at me.

"What was that?" I asked, feeling my face turn red.

"Your nose," he said. "It's humongous!"

I was caught off guard and didn't know what to do or say. I still wasn't sure I was hearing him right.

"You know, it's too early to be wearing a Halloween costume," he said, glaring at me.

I wasn't going to put up with this. I clenched my fist and took a step toward him. I'd teach him not to pick on me. Then a couple of other boys closed ranks with my tormentor.

"You're right, Jack," one of them said. "That is the biggest nose I've ever seen."

"Looks like he's got a banana stuck to his face," said the other boy.

At that moment, it seemed that everyone was laughing at me, and there was no way I could fight them all. I hung my head and walked away in humiliation.

Every day after that, someone took on the task to taunt me for my large nose—which had been so ordinary in Jordan; and if that wasn't enough, they ridiculed my accent or told me to go back to wherever I came from.

I was mocked for not having brand-name clothes to wear, especially sneakers. If you didn't have the right pair of sneakers, you were a nobody. My brothers and I were always neat and well-dressed, but my family had no money for Air Jordans or other sneakers that cost hundreds of dollars. Under the circumstances, I had inexpensive sneakers from Payless and a "large" nose. These factors were prominent in making me the ideal target for a good laugh.

Unusually enough, not everyone joined in. Some of the kids stood up for me, sat at the same table during lunch, and eventually became my friends. Unfortunately, there were enough bullies there to make my life miserable. I tried to pretend that their taunts didn't hurt me—but I often cried myself to sleep at night.

I recall being in a class where the students were drawing profiles of each other. We each took turns standing in front of a projector so that our sideways images were shown on the wall. A student would go up to the front of the class and copy the profile. Sure enough, the girl who drew my profile made it her mission to have fun with my nose; it appeared as if Pinocchio was on steroids. My nose went on and on. The class thought it was hilarious and laughed for what must have been five minutes, but it felt like an eternity. I sat there feeling humiliated, longing to disappear at that very moment and wishing that I could keep my face from turning red.

Until that moment, I tried my best not to let my mother and stepfather know I was being picked on at school. They must have known that something was going on with me because I had always loved learning before, and they could see how reluctant I was to go off to school in the morning. Occasionally, I took my troubles to God. I'd ask Him, "What would it be like if I was no longer alive? Then they couldn't make fun of my shoes or my nose." Like Hamlet, I struggled as I wondered which would be better, to live or to die. I never actually went so far as to plan my suicide or to think about how I would kill myself. I just wanted to get rid of the pain.

Off to Work at the Age of 12

It was during my horrible eighth-grade year that I discovered that one of my distant relatives owned a sandwich shop in Jersey City. To this day, I'm not sure what the family connection is. It's complicated. Regardless, the news was that "Cousin Jorge" was a nice guy, and he wanted me to come work for him. I was excited about it, because it would give me a chance to earn money and eventually purchase "cool" clothes. It would also give me an opportunity to help out my mother and stepfather.

One of the first things I did with my new-found wealth was go to the Foot Locker in Bayonne to look for a hot pair of shoes.

Immediately, my attention was captured by a pair of neon green Nikes. I tried to ignore them, but they were calling my name. I finally asked the clerk to bring me a pair of those sneakers and tried them on.

"Wow!" he said. "Those look good on you!"

Sold!

Those were the first Nikes I ever owned, and I wore them to school the next day. Obviously, I received myriad reactions, which were like tonic to my soul. Some people told me how great they looked. And others teased me with lines like, "You're going to blind us with those colors."

I didn't mind that kind of teasing. Those shoes may not have been your favorite color, but I finally got the famous check mark on the side of my "kicks".

Back at the sandwich shop, it was a hustle. Every afternoon, as soon as school was out, I'd head directly to work until late at night, also working every weekend. I missed so many picnics and birthdays, and to this day we have very few photos of me during those ruthless four years. I was always working!

It was hard work, and I quickly discovered that my boss wasn't such a nice guy after all. In fact, he had a terrible temper. He yelled at me—and everyone else who worked for him—all day long. Although he did not hit other employees, I often received a hard hit on the head from that heavy ring he wore. I guess he felt like it was all right to hit me because I was an immigrant child who needed the job, and, until the age of 16, I was effectively his property.

Oddly enough, my family thought Jorge was a great guy—and he was, when he wasn't at work. When you talked to him at a family get-together, he appeared to be the nicest guy you'd ever want to meet.

Friendly. Funny. Kind. Gracious.

On the job, he was dreadful—resembling Dr. Jekyll and Mr. Hyde.

It seemed to me that there was no end to this anguish. Sometimes, I lay in the darkness in my room at night, crying myself to sleep, long after everyone else was deep in slumber, envisioning the day I'd turned sixteen and obtain my freedom, get my working papers from school and secure a job that was less abusive and paid the minimum wage.

Until then I remained, as I liked having some spending money of my own, and I was content that I was able to provide my mother a helping hand. You see, every Friday I would get paid in cash and take half of that money to give it to my mother. I think the first few weeks I only kept transportation money for myself. Later, I gradually worked up to keeping half of my salary and sharing the rest. It felt so good; it was the least I could do for her.

At work, everyone reaches a boiling point; mine came when my boss became irate about a trivial matter and began calling me insulting names that had to do with my family's heritage. He continued on to speak ill of my mother, disrespecting her and impugning her character because she had given birth to a loser like me.

That was it! He could berate me as much as he wanted to, but I wasn't going to let him speak about my mom like that.

I yanked off my apron, wadded it up and threw it at him.

"I'm outta here," I said, and walked out the door.

"Issa, wait."

"I quit!" I shouted over my shoulder. I had fantasized about the day I would say these two words. I wasn't going to wait around and have more abuse heaped on me. Especially not for a measly $3 an hour. I kept going.

"Come back," he shouted. "Don't act like a baby!"

Before I even got home, his mother had called my mother, told her that I had quit, and asked her to talk me into coming back. Apparently, she went on about what a good worker I was, how much her son had come to rely on me and said several other nice things that had never once been said to my face. She also went on about how much pressure he was under, and that she hoped I would understand that this sometimes caused him to lose his temper.

I didn't buy it. Even though I understood that it could be tough to run your own business, that didn't give him the excuse to be cruel and vile all the time.

I didn't think he would ever really change, but when I spoke to him, he agreed to try, so I went back to work. After that, things weren't perfect, but they were slightly better. When I decided to walk away from the abuse it earned me respect. I stayed at the sandwich shop until I turned sixteen.

CHAPTER 8

THE
HEARTBREAK

Ketty, Ketty, Ketty

It was about this time that I met my dream girl. I say "dream girl" not only because she was unequivocally splendid in beauty, but because this masterpiece of creation saw something handsome about me. Yes, me. The immigrant boy with a giant-sized nose and burned neck. She was dazzlingly angelic, attentively compassionate and extraordinarily captivating. This was my first girlfriend, Ketty.

From very early on in our relationship I wanted to marry this girl. She was beautiful, smart and way out of my league. In fear of losing her, I assured myself that she was the one for me. Perhaps my assurance and enthusiasm frightened her a bit because I wasted no time in telling her that we'd be married one day.

Although I didn't go to Ketty's high school, a mutual friend introduced us in an online chat room. This was during the excitement of America Online; I was 15 years old and chatting away. I quickly found out, after just a few phone conversations, that I had hit the jackpot. The sound of her voice was serenely soothing, and I felt a degree of candid care in her conversations. I couldn't wait to meet her.

The only problem was that I wasn't sure she'd like me in person. I worried about the size of my nose and the acne on my face—maybe everything would end as soon as we met. For this reason, I didn't initiate our first face-to-face meeting until we had talked a number of times over the phone. In many of these conversations, I read her poetry I had written.

I vividly remember the first day we met. I was so nervous that I could hear and feel my heart beating out of my chest. Although it was at the movies with friends, we actually did not meet until the movie was over and we were standing outside the theater at Newport Mall in Jersey City.

That day felt as if God had allowed me to take a peek into my future, and it was magnificent. I was convinced that I had met my wife. Although I was only 15 years old, I had a gut feeling. For all I know, I felt like this because a dream-girl liked me during my lowest level of self-esteem. Or perhaps that's how every teenager feels about their first girlfriend.

After the movie, we took a walk by the park and talked at length. I mustered up all the courage I had and placed my hand on her shoulder. She played it cool and we kept walking and talking. I finally said goodbye to Ketty but, part of me wished I had the courage to kiss her instead.

Yet after that day, I began to have a new level of confidence. My fears and doubts about myself began to ease away. I was a more self-assured young man.

Ketty was—and is—beautiful on the inside and out, a brilliant girl with a light olive complexion. Her brown eyes mesmerized me, and I had to turn away to maintain my composure.

It wasn't only her physical beauty that attracted me to her. I knew before I actually met her face-to-face that she had an incredible personality, with a fun sense of humor, a quick wit and a laugh that made me feel good all over. How I enjoyed spending time with her on the telephone!

I also knew that Ketty was extremely bright. She went to a private high school in Jersey City with a strong college-prep program. The school wasn't easy to get into, and the tuition was high—but Ketty won a full scholarship and was one of the school's top students.

Upon graduating from high school, she won a full academic scholarship to St. Peter's University and then went on to pursue her master's degree in social work at Rutgers University. Her goal has always been to make people's lives better.

But let me not get ahead of myself.

I remember going to Ketty's church a few times and meeting her pastor. Even though I wasn't a church-goer, I always had a reverence and respect for God that my mother had instilled in me—so although the services were in Spanish, and I really didn't understand a word, I behaved respectfully.

Ketty told me that the people she knew were impressed that although I looked like a "bad kid," I listened, closed my eyes during the prayer and didn't act like a "tough guy." As one of them told her, "He wasn't dressed like he belonged here, but he acted like he belonged here."

Now, at this time I was approaching my 16th birthday. This was a big deal to me because it meant that I would be able to close my chapter at the sandwich shop and go out and get a "real" job making more money.

Ketty decided she wanted to do something special for my birthday, so we agreed that we would go to the World Trade Center in Manhattan on the weekend following my birthday. It never happened.

Four days before our date, on my 16th birthday, Tuesday, September 11, 2001, Al Qaeda terrorists flew jet airliners loaded with innocent passengers into the Twin Towers of the World Trade Center, killing over 2,900 people, injuring more than 6,000 others and causing more than $10 billion in damage. It was the worst attack on America ever. It stunned and saddened our entire nation. I took it especially hard because this monstrous act took place on my birthday, and it was carried out by terrorists with origins from the Middle East.

After that terrible day, I noticed that a lot of people had a different way of looking at me. They seemed to be wondering if I was "one of them".

I hoped that the 9-11 attack wouldn't change anything between Ketty and me, but other problems were on the horizon.

I slowly disconnected from all my well-behaved friends and started to draw closer to the troublemakers in school. I kept this a secret from Ketty because I did not want to expose her to my new gangster friends. It helped that we did not go to the same high school.

Then, on Tuesday November 20th, 2001, Ketty decided to break up with me, although she didn't tell me why. She simply told me she couldn't see me anymore, and she lived up to her word.

I loved Ketty and, as I said earlier, I just knew I was going to marry her. She was so beautiful, gentle and caring. Everything about her touched my heart.

I was devastated when she broke up with me, and though I considered myself a tough guy, I cried and cried. My mom came to me and tried to comfort me. "If she's going to be your wife, God will bring her back," she told me. "But in the meantime, you're young, and you have a lot to learn and a lot to do. You just wait. Everything is going to be okay."

I wasn't okay. When Ketty broke up with me, she completely removed herself from my life. It seemed final. She wouldn't return my calls. She ignored notes I sent her. She wouldn't have anything to do with me. I didn't hear a word from her.

I felt it was because I was inadequate in some way. I thought about all those kids who had bullied me, who had made fun of me because of my big nose and my accent. They must have been right about me. And then, too, I was from the Middle East just like those Al Qaeda killers. No wonder Ketty didn't want to be with me. I also drew a connection to how she was a church girl looking for God, while I was drifting as far away from Him as I could.

Unfortunately, I dealt with this perceived rejection by hanging around with the wrong crowd. Drinking. Fighting. Getting involved in mischief. I needed to belong, and my gang-banger friends welcomed me into their family.

Ketty's apparent rejection of me was among the worst pain I had ever experienced. Although we dated for only four months, nothing compared with the emotional agony I felt. I had been hurt and angry when my parents sent me off to boarding school in Jordan, but that was nothing like this.

Maybe church would heal?

It was about this time that a friend of mine invited me to come to a youth meeting at his church.

For a number of reasons, I hadn't been inside a church for quite a while. For as long as I remember, I was constantly working on Sundays. More so, I was not welcomed at the last church I had attended, so I decided it wasn't for me. The dirty looks I received from people who didn't like the way I was dressed sealed my decision. For some reason, I thought this time would be different, but it wasn't.

Was I experiencing rejection from the church too? Picture a young boy walking in and the youth group leader glaring right at him. He marches over and tells him that he needs to talk to him. Then he goes on to give him an extremely negative fashion critique. Unfortunately, that was my experience.

He didn't like the headband I wore. My clothes were too baggy. He didn't approve of the way I wore my hair.

"You can't come to church looking like that," he told me.

"Fine," I said. "I won't." And I left, vowing that I'd never go back to church.

I had always believed in God from the time I was a small child, and when the church rejected me, it was almost as if He was rejecting me too. It felt like every place of refuge did not want me. My dad, my job, my new country, my girlfriend, my school and even God himself.

For now, I began a new job at Dunkin' Donuts in Jersey City, following the footsteps of my mother and older brother Jacob.

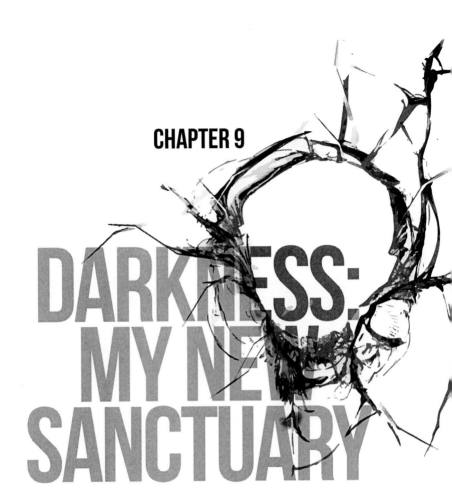

CHAPTER 9

DARKNESS:
MY NEW
SANCTUARY

Got Plans

I finally found it! I found acceptance in a group of people that many think of as unproductive members of society. However, when you get to know them, you realize that they're not what they're made out to be. They are just drifting through life, without any real plans or goals. They live for today and may not think too much about tomorrow. These negative qualities are products of their environment more than a product of their hearts. Once you were part of their group, they were going to defend you from danger. They would stick up for you and care for you no matter what. They may have a lot of things wrong, but they know what friendship is about.

This group might be considered a gang—but they weren't out there shooting people, dealing drugs, or causing unimaginable pain to others. In reality, it was a group that protected its members from unfair fights such as "getting jumped". Getting jumped means you were beaten by a group of attackers, not a one-on-one fight. It's usually done for adventure and excitement, but it puts the victim at a disadvantage.

I was pleased when a member asked me if I wanted to join the group. Of course, I did. I'd had been longing to belong. "What do I have to do?"

"You have to fight us," he answered.

"Us?" I asked. "Who is us?"

He smiled. "All of us."

He wasn't quite telling the truth. I didn't have to fight all 20 of them—just five guys from the gang, all at the same time. The idea was to see if the prospective new member—in this case me—had the guts to get up and fight back after he was knocked down, or if he would just lie there and give up. Anyone who wouldn't stand his ground wasn't accepted in this newly formed gang.

If I'd had any thoughts that these guys might take it easy on me, they were knocked out of me in a matter of seconds.

There was no dancing around or sizing each other up. They moved in and one of them smashed me in the mouth as hard as he could, splitting my lip.

Before I could react, another guy hit me in the eye, sending me sprawling to the ground.

I jumped back up and the brawl was on.

I ducked a punch and landed three quick blows on another boy, sending him staggering backwards. As I moved in to finish him off, someone stunned me with a hard punch to the midsection.

I don't know how long the fight continued, but it seemed like hours.

Nor do I remember how many times I was knocked down and got back up, but I know it was at least five. For the most part, I held my own. I knocked down other boys as many times as I was knocked down—but still, it was five against one, so I took the worst beating—and most of the damage was inflicted by one of the guys who was much bigger than the rest of us. He was several inches taller than me, with muscular arms and a broad chest. Having him in the fight was like having a heavyweight champion in the ring with a bunch of welterweights, and I still shudder when I remember how hard he hit me.

I could see it in my friends' eyes that they didn't really want to beat me like this, but they felt it was what they had to do. It was the law of the gang and they were compelled to follow it, and I understood. This beating was a lot different from the beating I'd taken four years earlier. The first beating was designed to make me go back to "my country". The second was a "welcome home" beating. Secretly, I didn't mind the latter, as I was craving acceptance at any cost.

When the fight finally reached a conclusion, we were all bloody and bruised. One of my eyes was black and swollen almost shut, I had a fat lip and a bloody nose, and I was in a lot of pain. Despite all of that, I felt only joy and elation as my homeboys gathered around, praising me for my valiant fight and welcoming me to the group.

What a thrill it was to find the acceptance I had longed for all these years. At that moment, there was nothing more important to me than the gang.

Now that I was in the group, I officially saw myself as a tough guy, and so did everybody else at school. I proudly wore the gang's color of gray—including a gray bandana. I also developed a hard stare to show everyone how tough I was, and most people stepped to the side when they saw us coming. We weren't bullies. We didn't push people around or start fights, but everybody knew we wouldn't back down from a confrontation. We were called "V" for Vigilantes, and the bullies left us alone because they knew that if they picked on one of us, they would have to answer to all of us.

One day, several of us were playing basketball in a park when we saw a guy who seemed to be in his mid-30s yelling at a boy of perhaps twelve. We didn't really know what he was so angry about, but he kept spewing profanity at the boy, calling him names and threatening to teach him a lesson. His behavior was way out of line, and the boy wasn't putting up any resistance. He seemed to be terrified.

Now remember that most of the boys in V had been bullied at one time or another. We hated to see anyone being picked on, especially by someone much bigger and stronger. One of our friends was so upset that he yelled at the older guy and told him to leave the kid alone.

Instead, he started swearing at us, telling us to mind our own business or we'd be in deep trouble. He should have been smarter than that. Like I said, he was bigger and stronger than any of us, but there were 15 of us and just one of him.

More words were exchanged, and the next thing I knew, our friend was going toe to toe with the older guy, and then the brawl was on. Our opponent was tough, and he knocked a few of us down, but we got back up and resumed the fight. I know it wasn't fair to gang up on the guy like that, but in our defense, I think we all saw in him every bully who had ever taunted us.

The problem for us was that he was just as crazy as we were. Instead of turning and running away, he fought like a tiger and he wouldn't give up. He just kept punching, kicking and threatening us. That's when I saw a piece of lumber lying on the ground. It was a 4x4 about six feet long, that must have been left behind by a construction crew working near the park. I picked it up and swung it at him as hard as I could, busting open the right side of his head. The man staggered away, with blood pouring down his face.

At that instant, we heard sirens in the distance. Had someone called the police? We scattered in different directions, running as fast as we could go. I couldn't believe what I had done, and knew that if the cops caught me, I would probably go to juvenile hall. Hitting that guy with a piece of lumber was an act in opposition to every value my mother had ever tried to instill in me. My friends, on the other hand, thought I was a hero. As the story spread through school over the next few days, I became even more of a hero. Nobody was going to mess with me.

On my end, I loved having a "tough guy" image, and I started dressing the part. I started wearing a long platinum chain with a huge cross on it, like a rapper, and acting like I had a big chip on my shoulder—which I did. It was horrible for me because I was a guy who knew what it was like to be bullied and picked on. Now I became this guy who could bully and pick on others—and I did. It was like I was trying to get even with the world for what had happened to me when I first came to America.

One rainy day I came home from school and found Hanna, my younger brother, pulling wet, muddy books and papers out of his backpack.

"What happened?" I asked.

He sighed. "Some kid grabbed my backpack, took everything out and threw it into the street—in the middle of all this rain."

"Why did you let him do that?"

"Because he's bigger than me?"

"Did you try to stop him?"

"I tried," my brother answered, "but he's a really big guy. Besides, his friends were with him."

"Can you identify him?" I asked.

"Of course."

"Well, tomorrow morning we're going to be waiting for him in front of your school, and we'll make sure this never happens again."

We did as I said and caught the boy and a couple of his buddies as they walked to school.

"I heard you've been picking on my brother, who is obviously half your size, you fat @$$!" I said.

One of his friends jumped in front of him to protect him, punched the guy in the face as hard as I could, and he went down. I stood over him, threatening to punch him again if he got back up—and the other boys backed away. Like most bullies, they wanted no part of someone who was willing to fight back. "If anyone messes with my brother, I'll #*%&! kill him," I snarled.

They all told Hanna they were sorry and that it wouldn't happen again.

Apparently, as soon as they got into the school, they went to the principal's office and reported that I, a high-schooler, was threatening to kill an eighth grader.

As soon as I got to Bayonne High School, I was interrogated by Mr. Merce, my vice principal. Even though I explained to Mr. Merce what had happened, that I was sticking up for my brother, and wasn't serious about killing the guy, I was suspended for ten days. My mother did not know what to do about me. She'd talk to me, but it didn't work, so she'd pray and pray and pray.

I was accepted into a lifestyle of darkness and it felt good. I couldn't see the light, even if I wanted to, I was getting too comfortable in the dark.

That summer, right before Hanna joined us as a freshman at Bayonne High School, I asked him and Jacob to join me in V. They both agreed without objection.

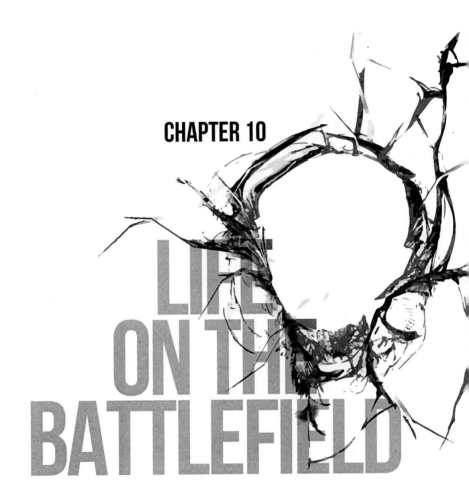

CHAPTER 10

LIFE
ON THE
BATTLEFIELD

The Braids

A few weeks into the school year, a boy ran up to Hanna and threatened to beat him up if he didn't take off that gray bandana. When I heard about it, I was furious. I don't know why, but my blood would boil every time someone picked on Hanna. I think it was because I saw him as the 12-year-old version of myself.

I knew who the kid was. He was in my class, another bully picking on someone younger than himself. This time, I planned to confront him and beat his behind, so I asked Hanna and Jacob to meet me for backup.

"Did you threaten to beat my brother yesterday?"

"What if I did?" He was trying to act tough, but he was also backing away. "It's none of your business."

He was going to be sorry for talking to me like that.

I moved forward and hit him in the mouth. Before he could respond, I charged at him again and tackled him to the floor. Then I was on top of him, hitting him again and again.

It only took a minute for school security guards to arrive. They pulled me off the other kid and told me to calm down. They held me for a minute or two while I struggled against them. One of the security guards, Ms. Diaz, who knew me, as I was friends with her brother, Nicholas, told me with a serious but gentle voice to calm down. Although Ms. Diaz was upset with me, I felt that deep down she was secretly proud of me for standing up for my little brother.

As soon as I gave the impression that I had calmed down, they let go of my hands momentarily, and I took full advantage of the opportunity, ran back at the kid and started hitting him again. That's how angry I was. It didn't take much to make me fly into a rage. That particular incident earned me another ten-day suspension. Mom felt more helpless. She only knew to pray fervently, asking God to bring me back to my senses.

I'm not proud of any of this. It bothers me to think about what a monster I was in those days. I convinced myself that I was fighting for all of the right reasons—like trying to protect my little brother—but I was an angry young man who was always ready to use my fists at the slightest provocation. The only way I knew how to handle a bully was to be a bully.

Driving in the Dark

I was determined to do what I wanted to do, no matter what the consequences might be. On one particular night, I decided to take the family car out for a spin; I did not have a driver's license. I took my mom's car keys and headed out for a short drive.

I hadn't gone too far when I realized that I didn't know how to turn on the headlights. I looked all over the dashboard but couldn't see any sort of knob or lever to push or pull.

I was driving slowly and carefully so as not to attract attention—but I could not find those lights.

"They've got to be here somewhere," I muttered to myself, just as I passed a black and white police cruiser.

"No, please. . ." I uttered to myself.

Too late. The officer began flashing his lights and got right behind me.

I kept on driving, but not for long. Instead, I drove around the block, back to my house, with the police car following me all the way. Then I pulled over.

I was dealing with a policeman with a good sense of humor. I told the cop, "Please don't tell my mom about the pack of Newports." He let me dispose of the cigarettes under the car.

When my mom and stepfather came running out of the house to see what was going on, he good-naturedly told them, "You better keep your eye on this one. He's a troublemaker."

He didn't give me a ticket—or even a warning. I had avoided serious trouble. When I saw the look in my mother's eyes, I knew I was breaking her heart, and I felt terrible about it.

It had to be my mother's prayers that kept me out of jail during those years. Although hitting the guy with the piece of lumber was probably the worst act any of us ever committed, some of the boys did get locked up for marijuana possession and other minor offenses.

I remember one day, we got hold of a stash of counterfeit tens and twenties to spend around town. After breaking a fake $10 bill at the grocery store, I didn't try to pass any of the other counterfeit bills. It just didn't seem right to me to cheat anyone like that. Despite my attempts to be a tough guy, I still had an internal conflict between doing right and wrong. A spark from my mother's values instilled in my upbringing still burned deep inside of me.

It was a small spark, and I'm sure my mother was in agony for most of those 18 months when I was running wild. I know she sent up hundreds of prayers on my behalf—and I'll never know how many tears she cried for me. Almost every night, she sat up praying and waiting for me to come home.

Arabs Suck

One evening my sister Mariana came home beaten up by a new boy in the neighborhood. My stepfather knew how to leverage me in that condition.

The boy also keyed my stepfather's van with the words "Arabs Suck." Naturally, my stepfather was upset and went to tell the boy's mother what he had done. She gave him the biggest attitude. "Go #*%! yourself!" she shouted at him. "My son is under 18, and there isn't a thing you can do about it."

Frustrated, my stepfather called me and told me what had happened. I don't remember exactly what I did, but my stepfather does. He tells me that I wasted no time in locating and badly beating the kid that hurt my sister. The very next morning, that family had already left our neighborhood. My stepfather loves retelling this story to this day.

Although my relationship with my stepfather appeared normal, the truth was that I avoided calling him "dad" at all costs. I would run into him and greet him with a "Hello" and quickly get into another subject to avoid using the word "dad".

I respected my stepfather enough to acknowledge him, but the thought of calling him "dad" was too much for me. It felt equivalent to saying that my biological father was dead, and now I had a new father. I just couldn't do that. Although I hadn't seen my "real dad" in years, he was alive and well, living in Jordan. I didn't think there was room in my life for two dads. Therefore, I tried to avoid the issue as much as possible.

The New Leader

After nearly one year in the group, our gang leader and now close friend, Brian—who started this gang when he moved to Bayonne from Queens, New York—moved to a new city and high school. Before leaving, he publicly appointed me to be his successor, a move that all the other guys supported.

However, just as I was taking control of the group, I was also losing interest. Something else had captured my attention. Music. I had discovered a new, fresh style of music called hip hop, and I was crazy about it. I'm not talking about the commercial music you hear on the radio, but rather the underground music of the street—battle rap. It was often vulgar, dirty and violent, but I couldn't get enough of it. Nas, Big

Pun, DMX, Jay-Z, 2-Pac, Biggie Smalls and Canibus were among my favorite rappers during this time of 1998 to 2002. In 1999, Eminem released The Slim Shady LP, and I became an immediate fan. Perhaps Eminem showed me that you can be different and with enough skills, you can still succeed in this country.

I began writing my own songs and recording them on my computer at home. Thanks to a new video game MTV: Music Generator, I'd learned to make my own beats. Before long, I had notebooks full of lyrics and two dozen songs on my PC. Then I asked for my mom's help in putting all my songs on a CD. When I played her a few of the songs I'd written and recorded, she was less than thrilled.

"Why do you want to make music like this?" she asked. She was disappointed with all the profanity in the lyrics.

"Mom." I said. "You don't believe in me, do you? Don't you know that my music could make us rich someday? And when that happens, I'm going to buy you a big house to live in and take care of you."

When I told my mom, "You don't believe in me," it scarred her for years, given all that she had been through for her children.

Despite my mother's objections to the music, she swallowed her pride and helped me replicate and package 100 CDs, which I took to school and sold to my classmates for $5 apiece. I sold them all in a couple of weeks and made a profit. The CDs cost me about $1.00 to make, giving me an eighty percent margin on each sale.

This experience opened my mind to the opportunities available in business.

By now the gang had grown to about 40-45 guys. I decided to cut it down to a smaller group of guys who shared my interest in music. I wound up with 16 who had some interest in music. All of them could either sing, dance, rap or play an instrument. We called ourselves The Reapers, and my stepbrother Shadee made beats for us and even made us our own logo. The gang had become a music crew.

All of us were still in high school, except for my best friend, Steven, who was six years older than me. Like me, he was very much into music, and we hit it off from the first time we met. But not everyone wanted to be my friend.

There was one guy in particular, a rapper who called himself "Dave" who really had it in for me. Dave wanted to prove that he was the best rapper in Bayonne High School.

His opportunity to show what he could do came about halfway through our senior year of high school. For some reason, all the students had gathered in the auditorium. If memory serves me correctly, we were waiting for a pep rally to start.

Dave saw me, stood up and started spitting lines about me. He let me have it, and I have to admit he was pretty good. He started out attacking me because, according to him, he was the better rapper. Then he went after my ethnic background and the size of my nose and labeled me a terrorist.

I sat there and took it, my face red with embarrassment. My friends wanted me to fight back. "Come on man, we know you've got bars. . . let 'em have it!" I just couldn't. Dave was the sort of guy who made up rhymes on the spot. Some of them were crude and clumsy, but he got away with it. I knew that if I tried to do that, I'd only embarrass myself.

My songs were poetry. I've spent hours writing them, not only did they flow perfectly, they needed to be thoughtful and logical. He had me this time, and it seemed that he also had the entire student body in the palm of his hand. They were rocking back and forth with him, oohing and then ahhing as he blasted me with one of his lines.

I wanted to disappear.

Just like Eminem in his film *8 Mile*, I used my frustration to write back. So, as soon as I got home, I began working on a track for Dave. I hit back real hard. I spent the whole evening on it, recorded it on a CD, and took it to school the next day. Everyone who heard it loved it—and that was just about everybody. Then I had a copy hand-delivered to Dave himself.

I didn't hear anything about it until a couple of weeks later, when I was at a birthday party for my cousin Jackie! I didn't think he'd be invited, but Dave was there with his usual entourage. He didn't say a word to me, but one of his pals snapped the chain off my neck as he walked past. "You don't mess with my boy, Dave," he threatened me. I looked at my two friends and signaled them to cool down with my hand gestures. I swallowed my pride because I didn't want to ruin Jackie's party. I picked up my chain and played it cool. We were supposed to keep the rivalry on tracks, not real life. At that point, I stopped my attempts to stir things up. It may have hurt my reputation, but I didn't give it any further thought.

After that, our contention just evaporated.

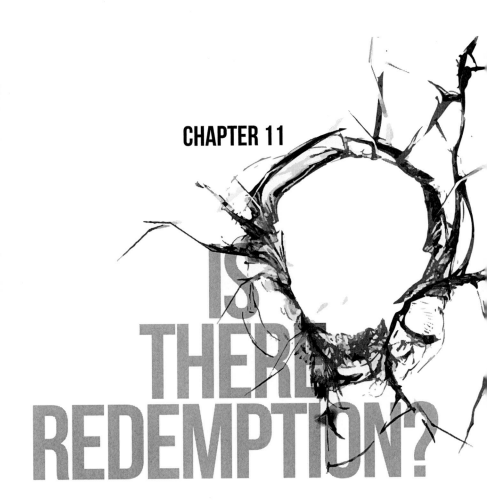

CHAPTER 11

IS THERE REDEMPTION?

Winter Camp 2002

Everyone who knew me thought I was a gangster.

No one saw me when I was all alone in my room, late at night and unable to sleep.

I thought of all the fights I had been in, all the boys I had beaten so severely. When it came to a fight, I didn't just want to knock a guy down, I wanted to destroy him. I was merciless.

There were so many other things I'd done. I wasn't exactly a criminal, but I was nearly there. My friend Brandon asked if I would help him sell drugs and start making some good money, but I was worried about getting caught by the police. So I put that decision on hold.

Because of what I'd done, I wondered if I could ever be a loving husband and father. Could I treat my future wife with tenderness and respect, the way she deserved to be treated? Would I be able to teach my own children to know the difference between right and wrong, and always choose the right?

Would God be able to forgive me? Is He real? Can my life have meaning? I didn't know the answers to questions like these that tormented me, so I tried my best to push them out of my mind. I knew I was lost, but I distracted myself with work.

I loved my job at the Dunkin' Donuts/Baskin Robbins shop. My bosses were good to me, especially because my entire family worked there. For the first time in my life, I was making what I considered to be decent money, the real minimum wage of $5.15 an hour. I had worked my way up from $3.00 an hour to $3.50 in those four long years at my previous job, so starting at $5.15 was nice.

I worked most weeknights and all weekends. On Saturdays, my mother and I shared a shift. It was awkward at first, but when I saw her dedication, the experience changed for the better.

I was fascinated by the line of customers that would form just for my mother. These customers would only want her to make their coffee. It was bizarre to me because Dunkin' Donuts has a machine that keeps the tate universal by regulating how much milk and sugar is dispensed in a cup of coffee as per the customer's request to keep the taste universal. How did her coffee taste better? I had no clue.

So I asked my mother, "Why do you have these people requesting you? Coffee is going to taste the same no matter who makes it."

She smiled and said "You're right! The coffee is exactly the same, but how you serve it can change its taste"

"Huh?"

"When you serve it with your heart and a warm smile, it tastes better. When you serve it in a rush and with a bad attitude, it tastes bad".

My mother understood that the taste of coffee is actually the same, but a spirit of hospitality sweetens the experience. It kept customers coming back for her.

This short lesson on customer satisfaction may have given me the foundation I needed to build my career.

On Friday nights, I would see the same young people at around 7:00 p.m. every week. I have to admit that my attention was especially captured by the girls who smiled back each time I served them. Apparently, they were members of the church group from across the street. I guess I had developed a "thing" for church girls from my experience with Ketty.

When one of the girls asked me, "Why don't you join us next Friday? It's really a lot of fun," I decided that maybe I could ask my boss for a Friday evening off.

After doing that, I called up some of my boys and told them, "Guess what? We're going to church on Friday."

They all said, "Okay." No one argued with me or asked me if I had lost my mind. If I wanted to go to church, they were all for it. They liked it even more when I told them we might be able to meet some attractive young ladies there.

"The last time I went to church, I got kicked out," I told them. "If the same thing happens this time, we can fight back."

My friends loved that idea.

It turned out there were five of us who went to the service the following Friday night, including my brother Hanna and my friends Steven, Branden and Winfield. We all dressed pretty much alike, which was the same way I had dressed when I had been thrown out of the last church I'd tried to attend—long white tee-shirt, baggy pants, doo-rag and a fitted hat. After all, that was the way I dressed, and I wasn't trying to impress anyone. I figured we were probably going to get into it pretty fast because we looked like tough guys, and that's pretty much what we were.

As soon as we walked through the door, we were approached by a man named Frank. I recognized him because he and his family were regular customers at the donut shop. "Here it comes," I thought, and braced myself for a confrontation.

"Issa!" he exclaimed with a huge smile on his face. "I'm so glad to see you! We've been hoping that we'd see you someday." He walked over, leaned in and gave me a warm hug. Not exactly what I expected.

"And these must be friends of yours. Welcome to Cityline, guys."

Frank handed us off to another usher, who also gave us a big, bright smile, and then led us down the aisle to our seats in the center of the auditorium. I didn't smile, and I had that flashy platinum chain around my neck. Everywhere I looked I saw welcoming smiles, even on the faces of those pretty girls I wanted to meet.

We sat down and listened politely while the youth leader gave a short talk. Much to my surprise, I found myself agreeing with him, and I liked his easy, friendly manner.

When he finished speaking, we all went into another room at the back of the church where there were ping pong tables, and a whole bunch of video games. We wound up having fun, and we didn't get into any trouble at all.

Toward the end of the evening someone asked me if I had a good time. When I said that I did, he said, "Then you're going to love what happens here on Sunday." Secretly, I was hoping to meet another angel like Ketty, but that did not happen.

I later asked my boss to have Sunday off because I wanted to go to church, he shook his head and laughed. "Where are you really going?"

"To church."

"Come on, really."

It took a while, but he finally realized that I was telling the truth, gave me the day off, and I went to church on Sunday morning. As a boy in Jordan I had attended two different churches. There was the Catholic Church, where the sermon was preached in Latin and I never understood a word of it. I knew when to stand up, when to sit down, when to kneel, when to cross myself, and that was about it. That was my mom's family's church in Aqaba. The other church was evangelical. They called themselves born again. My dad's family went there simply due to its proximity to their home.

What I heard at Cityline not only made sense, it had me thinking about my future. This church was different; the people were different. It had a mix of different ethnicities. The diversity in that congregation made me feel comfortable coming back. It was exciting to know that I was representing one of over fifty different ethnicities and nationalities.

At the end of his sermon, the pastor, Joshua Rodriguez, asked "If you want a personal relationship with Jesus, raise your hand". I knew that was what I wanted and needed, and my hand went up.

That's when he said, "If you raised your hand, I want you to come on down to the front for prayer."

Oh, I hadn't bargained on that. It was one thing to raise your hand in the air while everyone around you had their heads bowed and eyes closed. It was quite another thing to walk up to the front, where all eyes were on you and everyone could see exactly what you were doing. Thankfully, several people sitting near me stood up, stepped into the aisle and made their way forward. I thought, maybe it wouldn't be so bad if I wasn't the only one doing it. Even though I wasn't afraid of anything, it took every ounce of courage and strength I had to walk down that aisle. In fact, I felt like running to the front. My heart was pounding, and I also felt like running for the back door. Now I don't know what I said, but when I got back from that altar, I felt whole.

As soon as I got back to the donut shop, I told my boss I wanted to change my schedule. I needed to have Sunday mornings off so I could go to church. His eyes grew wide with surprise. He had been shocked that I wanted to go to church one time. But every week? He acted as if he had seen a miracle. I guess he had. He was glad to adjust my work schedule.

From then on, I went to church every Sunday. It was there that I kept thinking again and again about my future, what type of person I wanted to be and the profession I would pursue.

God or Friends?

Several weeks later, Pastor Rodriguez talked about how bad company destroys good character. As I sat there listening to him, it suddenly hit me that I couldn't go on living the way I did. I thought, I'm came to church because I wanted to be a better man and have good character. Yet I kept going back to my friends, hung out with them and did all the things I had done before. I knew I had to change. I had to completely commit or quit, or I could never have the peace I desired.

As soon as I got home from church that Sunday, I called my friend Steven and said, "You know what I learned today?"

"No. What?"

"That bad company destroys good character."

He didn't respond, so I went on. "It got me thinking about all these Sundays when I go to church. And I really want this change in my life."

"Go on."

"What I'm trying to say is that you're either with me or not," I said. "You're either going to come with me on this journey and try to live this new life, or I'll have to do it alone."

Steven was a dear friend. The last thing I wanted to do was hurt him. We had done some real damage together and I didn't want to disconnect from him. I just wanted to become someone more dynamic and not limit myself to music and parties.

We talked for another ten minutes or so and had a very respectful conversation.

"I'm really happy for you, man," he told me. "I really am. I'm proud of you and I applaud you. But I can't promise you that I can do what you're doing. I want you to go ahead and do what you have to do."

That conversation with Steven was a turning point. After that I began pursuing my faith with my whole heart and building a brand-new life for myself. I quit hanging out with the wrong crowd. I got rid of all the songs and lyrics I had written. They were not compatible with the new vision I had for my life, so I destroyed them. The friendships that were not moving me forward, I left behind. Everything changed for me.

That wasn't the end of my relationship with Steven, but it was some time before I saw him again. He actually came to church for a while, but it didn't impact him the way it did me. On the other hand, I'm happy to say that Hanna felt the same way I did, and he became an important partner on the road of faith. Hanna and I have always had a special relationship—almost like twins—and it was great for me to know that my brother was also now my spiritual brother.

CHAPTER 12

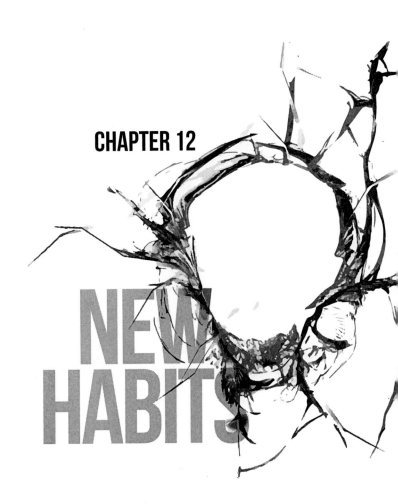

NEW HABITS

Yoohoo

I learned that the sanctuary opened at 5:00 a.m. every morning and I wanted to be there as often as I could. It was a safe place to keep thinking and pray. I would take the bus and go, sometimes with my sister Mariana and step-sister Doaa. I would often see Pastors Joshua and Paula spending time praying for the people from the church.

They would pray for the city, state, nation and world. They covered government, the economy, the arts and entertainment, education, and always prayed for the next generation. I did not realize you can pray about everything. Pastor Paula noticed a hunger and thirst to learn in us and asked me and my sisters to join her and Pastor Joshua for some morning teachings. It was a very special season, where we got to know this pastoral couple on a more intimate level. What a model of marriage that I wanted for my life!

I often went to Pastor Rodriguez to ask him questions about my new journey and he was generous with his time. I deeply admired him. I remember asking him, "What do I have to do to become a pastor?" He patiently and thoroughly took me through the process, "Some study to be pastors and go on to be pastors. Others feel a strong call to be pastors and become pastors. I say it's best to have both, a sense of calling along with the education. Let's also consider the intentions…" He went on and shared a lengthy and insightful view of the topic. I wanted to know more as I evaluated what I wanted to do down the road.

I was so excited about the church family and the message of love that was taught. I was still working at the donut shop, and the boss, Mr. Lee, started calling me Father Issa, teasing me about the change he noticed in my life.

My grades midway through my senior year had all been D's and F's. Now, after turning my life around, they improved to A's. A sharp upward curve brought my average just above the minimum GPA required to graduate high school. The decisions I made to focus on growing changed the trajectory of my life.

I began to accompany the pastor on several speaking engagements, helping him in any way I could and learning the work of ministry. That wasn't very long after 9/11, and people from the Middle East were not in great favor in the United States. Yet the pastor took a young man from Jordan to travel with him. That was an honor I will always remember. This sparked a desire in me to serve in any capacity. If anyone needed me, I rolled up my sleeves—let's go!

The Bus Card

So many things were happening that were helping me learn to be patient and trust in God rather than always take matters into my own hands.

One instance, Hanna came home from school and complained, "Some guy stole my bus card."

"What?" I asked. "How did that happen."

"I had it," Hanna explained, "and this guy says, 'Hey, I really like the looks of that card. Can I see it for a minute?' When I objected, he said, 'Come on, I'll give it right back to you.'"

Of course, when Hanna handed him the card, he grabbed it and ran back to the other side of the room, where his friends all began admiring "his" brand-new bus card and daring Hanna to try to get it back.

The loss of a bus card was a pretty big deal, because it was worth a bit of money. Without it, Hanna would have to pay a hefty price to get back and forth to school every day.

I could feel my blood starting to boil. My first inclination was to go find the thief and give him a good beating. I had done this kind of thing so many times before. Nobody was going to push my little brother around.

Then it hit me. I am different now.

"Hanna," I said. "There was a time when I'd go pound this guy."

He nodded, "I know."

"But I can't do that anymore."

"I know that, too."

We thought for a moment and then I said, "The only thing I can think of is to pray for him."

So that's what we did. Hanna and I sat down together and prayed that God would deal with him and that he would return the bus card. I admit that it was hard. Old habits die hard, and I still wanted to clobber the guy.

"Father God, wake this boy up! Right now, Speak to him. If you have to, scare him. Do whatever you do so he can feel terrible and bring this bus card back. We thank you in advance for what You will do. In Jesus' name, Amen."

The next day, Hanna came home from school, walked up to me and said, "Look what I have." He reached out and showed me what he held in his hand.

"Your bus card!" I said. "What happened?"

"The guy who took it walked up to me, handed it to me and said, 'Here's your bus card.'"

"That was it?" I asked.

"That was it."

The joy I felt at an answered prayer was profound. We didn't have to step up our vocabulary to be heard, we just had to step up our faith. My old way of handling the situation may have drastically set me back.

I knew that I was experiencing transformation. People began to ask me, "What happened to you? You changed." I would say that before

I changed the way I dressed and talked, change had been taking place on the inside. My outside appearance began to change after the total makeover I experienced inside.

Even though things were going well for me, my love life was another matter. After all this time, I still had feelings for Ketty, although it had been about two years since the breakup, and I hadn't heard a word from her.

Then one day, out of the blue, I got a call from Ana, one of Ketty's childhood friends.

"Issa, it's Ana! How are you?"

"Oh my God, Ana? I'm doing well," I said, with a surprised tone.

"I was just cleaning out some drawers and I came across your number. It's been a long time. How's Hanna doing? How's Jacob?"

She was thrilled to hear about all the changes that had come into my life since I started living a life more aligned with my faith, and said she'd love for us all to get together.

"Do you still hang out with Ketty, Victor and their family?" I asked.

"Of course, I see them all the time."

We talked on for quite a while, and then she asked me if I'd like to come over to Ketty's neighborhood to say hello to everyone.

"Sure, that sounds like fun. When did you want to do this?"

"Are you doing anything this afternoon."

The truth was that I didn't have many open afternoons, between work and college, but this was too important to pass up.

We wound up gathering in front of Ketty's house, although she wasn't there at first. I did meet with her brother Victor, discovered that he was now serving in their home church as a youth leader, and we had a fantastic time talking about God.

When Ketty finally joined us, my heart began beating so fast and so loud that I was afraid she could hear it. She seemed indifferent to me. She said hello, but there was little warmth in her greeting; it was awkward. I guess she was shocked to see me and it completely caught her by surprise, though there wasn't an expression of excitement anywhere on her face.

Then one Sunday evening at the start of the holiday season one of the youth group leaders came up to me and said, "Issa, we've got you on the schedule for Friday night in four weeks. Is that okay with you?"

I wasn't sure what he meant.

"On the schedule?" I asked.

"Yes, you know. On the schedule to preach."

My heartbeat immediately shot into overdrive, but I heard myself say, "Absolutely! I've been waiting for this."

It was true. I had been waiting and hoping that I'd be invited to share about all the transformation that I've been experiencing. Still, the thought of getting up in front of people made me nervous. I figured it couldn't be any harder than rapping in front of a tough crowd. The thing was, this time I had something really positive to share!

The next time I saw Pastor Rodriguez, I asked him if he was going to come hear me speak on a Friday night. He grinned at me and said, "Of course I'm going to be there. I wouldn't miss it for the world!" I knew he was a very busy man. He didn't make it to the youth meetings very often, and I figured he'd have something else to do on Friday night. It had never really occurred to me that I'd be speaking in front of such an accomplished speaker. The very idea upped my anxiety level a little bit, but it made me feel really good to see how much he cared. At that moment, I had this strange feeling that he'd become like a father to me.

Not too long before my speaking engagement came, I quit my job at Dunkin' and pursued an opportunity at Toys"R"Us.

I had really enjoyed my time at Dunkin' Donuts/Baskin Robbins, but moving away from serving food felt like a promotion even though the hourly wage was similar. Of course, the job there was only supposed to last through the Christmas season—when toy sales were through the roof—but I planned to prove myself invaluable so they'd keep me on long after the Christmas sales were over.

I didn't waste any time before inviting my new fellow employees and a couple of my supervisors to come hear me speak. I had developed a strong personality, and I didn't mind being in the limelight. Nonetheless, it wasn't about me this time. It was all about this man named Jesus who loved me, even as an immigrant.

I worked hard on my presentation and I invited everyone I knew. This included Victor and his youth group. At that time, Pastor Paula had assigned me to work with the children's ministry. Several kids ages 10-12 expressed interest in hip-hop music, and I was working with them on several songs that I had written that we'd eventually present at the church. I thought that it would be fitting to leverage this hip-hop performance to draw a larger crowd on the day I'd speak. A crowd would come out to support the children who participated and at the same time hear a message of change. This strategy coupled with my own efforts helped us draw approximately 80 people as the audience. I was pleased to see Victor and his youth group. As I scanned his group, I noticed Ketty in the crowd and my heart accelerated.

To my surprise, the message was well received, and I was excited to see a huge response at the invitation to come forward for prayer. In fact, so many people came for prayer that there weren't enough ministers to pray with them. I noticed Ketty coming up for prayer too.

In the middle of all this excitement, I happened to catch a glimpse of the pastor's face, and I could tell that he was perturbed about something. He looked almost angry, and my heart sank. Had I done something wrong? I thought back over the entire evening, and I couldn't think of anything, but maybe I had blown it.

After the service wrapped up, I waited around to talk to him in private. He seemed shocked when I asked if I had done something wrong.

"No!" he said. "You did a great job, son. Why do you ask?"

"Well," I admitted, "I thought you were upset about something."

He looked puzzled for a moment, and then his eyes widened as he said. "The only thing I was upset about was that we weren't ready."

"Ready?"

"For the response. Our ushers weren't prepared. We should have had more people lined up and ready to pray with all the kids that came up. Delay can be dangerous in a situation like this. We've got to be ready to respond immediately."

He smiled. "You did well tonight. I'm proud of you, son." The word "son" landed on me like a quiet bomb, helping me realize the need I had for a father.

His encouraging words were a great finish to an incredible evening and cemented a mentorship relationship that would go on for decades. This man left behind a lucrative wall street career to serve as a full time pastor; something about that fascinated me.

CHAPTER 13

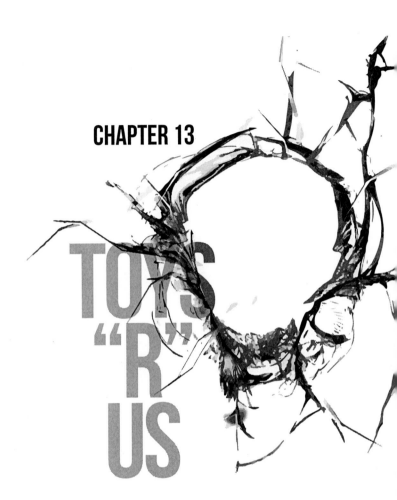

TOYS "R" US

Discovering my gifts

By this time in my life, I was on a mission to improve my life in every way. I always had an appetite for learning, but it drastically intensified since I had been living this new life. I believed that God wanted great things for me, so I desired great things for myself. I couldn't sit back and watch the world go by.

As the calendar moved toward the holidays, I saw that Toys"R"Us was hiring seasonal workers.

I had spent several years working in the food service industry, first for Jorge, and then for the Dunkin' Donuts/Baskin Robbins shop. I had enjoyed my time at the donut shop, but I wanted to grow further. I was confident that I could make my mark as a salesman but needed some experience and figured that Toys"R"Us was my chance to get involved in the retail world.

At this time, I continued making decisions that would change the trajectory of my life. I cut my long hair, changed my entire wardrobe and began wearing a suit and tie. So, I overdressed for the interview, but it seemed to work. They hired me on the spot.

It wasn't long before I was working at Toys"R"Us as a cashier, along with several other new hires. I knew that we were all there for Christmas, but, as I mentioned earlier, I intended to make myself invaluable. My plan was to still be working there long after the holidays had passed.

To sell or not to sell...

One of the first things I noticed, after getting hired at Toys"R"Us, was that the employees wore three types of branded shirts. The temporary, seasonal employees like me wore blue shirts. Most of the permanent employees wore red shirts. Some in management wore black shirts.

Now there weren't many of those black shirts. They were a badge of honor, a sign that you were one of the elite members of the Toys"R"Us team. A black shirt represented years of effort, success and leadership.

I also discovered that Toys"R"Us made a considerable profit by selling an insurance product. We were told to push a brand-new product called a BPP—Buyer Protection Plan. This was, in essence, an insurance policy that cost $2.99 and up. If you bought an electronic toy that cost $50, $75, or any amount, and it broke, the insurance policy would cover its replacement. It was a good idea, especially if you were buying expensive video games.

The pep talk went something like this:

"How many Buyer Protection Plans are we going to sell today? We need to sell at least twenty. If each of us sells just one of them, we will have met our goal. If everybody sells two, we'll double our goal!"

Management wasn't presenting it to us the right way. If they had told us how the protection plans worked—that they could save our customers a lot of money by replacing their broken toys, we probably would have been more enthusiastic. We weren't even told why the goal was so important. It meant nothing to most of us.

Still, they kept on talking about that goal of 20. At first, I wasn't really comfortable with the product, but then I read the pamphlet that explained it. Then I read it again. The more I understood it, the more I felt good about it.

The wonderful thing about these policies was that they protected consumers at a very small cost and yet, frankly, most of the time they weren't needed. At least they provided peace of mind. If you sold a policy and it was never used, then you were bringing in pure profit to the store. On those occasions when a toy broke, the policies prevented a lot of frustration for children and their parents. In other words, it was a win-win situation.

As much as we were reminded to sell these policies, most of the clerks sold none. This was because they never asked their customers if they wanted to buy one. Instead of seeing the benefit of the product, they just assumed people wouldn't be interested and didn't even ask. Or if they did ask, they did it in a quiet, low-key way as if it were an afterthought rather than something really important.

Their approach reminded me of the insecure boy who asks a pretty girl for a date by saying, "You wouldn't want to go out with me, would you?"

Not exactly the way to win a fair lady's heart.

As for me, I asked every one of my customers if they were interested in a warranty, and I presented it as a great new idea, which it was.

"Chances are, you'll never need it," I told them honestly. "But if you do, you'll be glad you have it."

Not long after that, I sold four of them in one day.

The next morning, one of the store managers came to me and said, "Listen, if you sell five of these by noon, I'll buy you lunch." Before you know it, various department managers were all challenging me to sell more of the BPPs, and I was selling enough that I had a free lunch every day.

I noticed that none of the other employees were even trying to sell the policies. In retrospect, I think they were afraid of rejection, and they didn't want to deal with that. They just wanted to stand at their registers, get the customers in and out of the store as quickly as possible, and hope that time to clock-out would hurry up and get there. They were saying "No" to themselves well before any customer had the opportunity to say "No" to them.

As for me, I tried not to take rejection personally. A "No" was not directed at me, it was directed at the product. I saw selling as a competitive game, and I loved it. Plus, it made me feel good to think that I was doing something that benefitted my customers. Because of this, I often sold 10, 15, or 20 Buyer Protection Plans a day. It was exhilarating.

CHAPTER 14

THE
BLACK
SHIRT

Why the Black Shirt?

One day there was a really bad snowstorm. It wasn't easy to make it in to the store that day, and it was unlikely that we'd have many customers. Still, I was there, and before the day was out, I had sold 45 Buyer Protection Plans. That had to be one for the record books, and I felt good. Other than that, I didn't think that much about it.

When I walked into the store the next morning, I was greeted by one of the department managers who told me, "Everybody's talking about you. You're the man!"

"Me? The man? What do you mean?"

"Haven't you seen the email?"

"Email, what email?" I had to remind him that I was a temporary employee, and as such, didn't even have an email address at the company.

He told me that corporate headquarters had sent out an email saluting me for selling 45 Buyer Protection Plans in the middle of a snowstorm.

When the store director, the big boss, heard all this, he told me, "You just got lucky, kid."

I knew he was trying to be funny, but it wasn't exactly the best way to motivate me. Or maybe it was, because his words fired me up, and I let him know it.

In fact, I told him that if I put my mind to it, I bet I could sell 100 of the protection plans in a single day.

He laughed so hard he snorted when he heard that.

"No way! You could never do that!"

I stood my ground, even though I wondered if I was overdoing it—just a little.

"Okay," he said. "Let's make a little bet. Let's see if you can sell 100 of them tomorrow."

"Tomorrow?" I repeated. "Well, okay, sure. As long as I can come in as early in the morning as I want to and stay until closing."

He shrugged, "Of course."

"And I want to be in the R-Zone." The R-Zone was a fenced-off area of the store where all of the electronics and video games were sold. Obviously, this was the best spot in the store to be selling Buyer Protection Plans.

"Anything else?"

"Yes. If I do sell 100 policies, what's in it for me?" I asked.

He shook his head. "Well, in the first place, you could never sell a hundred. But if you did, what would you want?"

"Your black shirt."

"My shirt?" He put his hands on his chest and leaned back, as if he didn't quite get it. "Why would you want my shirt?"

I shook my head. "Let me rephrase that. I want a black shirt like yours."

Now I could have asked for a raise. I wasn't making much more than minimum wage. I could have asked for a bonus. I don't really know what drew me to the black shirt, perhaps the shirt was a symbol of leadership and I wanted to be a leader. If I had that black shirt, maybe the other employees would listen to me and I could teach them to sell more—and care more.

"You've got a deal," he said. Then he added in a taunting tone, "But let me tell you. It's never gonna happen."

I took that personally. I couldn't understand why my boss would not encourage me to win. I thought maybe he saw that I would thrive from his negativity and wanted to push me to perform? Or he just did not want to see an immigrant boy get this type of attention. I wasn't sure.

By now, some of the other associates were getting into the action. Some were with the boss. They didn't think anyone could sell 100 policies in one day. Others were patting me on the back and telling me, "You're going to look great in that black shirt!"

When I got home from work that evening, I called on a new friend, Dan. He was one of the leaders at the church.

I told him the story and asked him if I was stepping out of bounds. Was I being unrealistic or overly optimistic thinking that God would help me sell 100 Buyer Protection Plans?

My friend didn't think so.

"There is no limit to what God can do through anyone who trusts in Him" he told me. "Besides, you sold 45 of these things during a blizzard. Just imagine what you can do on a normal day!"

When the doors opened for customers, I was at my register and ready to sell. It took me about 20 minutes to sell the first policy. Then I sold three to one gentleman. By about 10 o'clock, I had sold 20, but four per hour wasn't nearly enough. I had to pick up the pace. I kept selling during my normal break time. By 11 o'clock, I was up to 30. I relied on my fast eating skills I'd picked up at the sandwich shop, where I only had a 10-minute lunch break; so I shoved down a sandwich in only five minutes, because I wanted to keep selling. I kept a pad of paper beneath my register, and I marked off each purchase, like a prisoner marking off the days until he's finally set free.

All day long I was watching the clock. By 2 p.m. I had sold 60 policies. By 4 p.m. 72. By the time 6 o'clock rolled around I was still 20 policies from my goal. I had three hours to go and I had to sell seven policies per hour. Could I do it? I was tired and beginning to have my doubts, but I wasn't going to give up.

"I Made It!"

A couple minutes before nine o'clock I met my goal. Policy number

100 went to a nice couple from Bayonne who were shopping for their grandkids. And just as the store was closing, a pretty young woman bought number 101! I had done it!

I think I expected sirens to go off, confetti to fall from the ceiling and a band to start playing "We Are the Champions", but nothing of that sort happened.

I went home, exhausted from the long day, and got a good night's sleep. I was sure there would be a celebration of some type when I got back to the store in the morning. I envisioned everyone gathering around me as I was presented with a beautiful black shirt, perhaps even encased in a gorgeous frame.

I was wrong. As far as everyone else was concerned, it was just another day. The store director did not even acknowledge me.

I wasn't going to let him get away with it.

"Hey, where's my black shirt?" I asked.

"Black shirt," he answered. "What are you talking about?"

"Our bet," I told him. "I sold 100 of the consumer protection plans. Actually, one hundred and one."

"You did? Are you sure about that? I haven't even checked the records."

He went back into his office for a few minutes. Then he came out and said, "Kid, you really got lucky." He repeated it a couple of times for emphasis.

"It had nothing to do with luck," I protested. "I worked my butt off to sell those policies. And I feel like I did something great for you and the entire team."

He kept belittling my accomplishment, saying over and over again how lucky I was—but I wasn't about to listen to that.

"I want my black shirt," I said. "And if I don't get it, I'm outta here."

When he saw that I was serious about walking out the door his attitude changed.

"All right," he held up his hands in an appeasing gesture. "You've earned your shirt. Let me see what I can do."

He left the room for a few minutes, then came back carrying something in a plastic bag, and tossed it at me.

I opened it and found a wadded up, wrinkled, dirty black shirt. It was filthy, smelled like perspiration, and the aroma of someone's leftover lunch. It seemed to me that my boss was doing everything in his power to make it difficult for me to wear that shirt.

Even as he congratulated me on what I had done, he had to throw in a little barb. "You'll never do it again," he said.

But I had a plan. I took the shirt home, gave it to my mom and asked her if she could fix it up for me. By the time she worked her "mother's magic" on it, that shirt looked brand new.

When I walked into the store the next morning, wearing that shirt, all heads turned in my direction.

I could hear their whispers, "How did he get that black shirt?" "He must have done something incredible."

It was such a proud moment for me because my new shirt signified something important that I had learned about myself. I knew now that I could do anything I set my mind to.

That day, as I enjoyed wearing my black shirt, I sold 105 buyer protection plans!

I have no way of knowing, but I imagine that's a record that still stands. Of course, when I climbed into bed that night, I saw those darned policies when I closed my eyes. I dreamed I was selling them, and when I woke up the next morning, I felt like I hadn't slept at all, even though I knew I had.

A few weeks after I received the black shirt, a new director came to our store. He was intrigued by the fact that I was wearing a black shirt and asked around to find out how I got it.

Then, he called me into his office and asked me to tell him all about how I managed to sell these policies at an extraordinarily high rate. He seemed genuinely interested and impressed with my accomplishment.

"I'll tell you what I'm going to do. First, I'm going to make sure you get the best possible raise for your annual review—35 cents an hour. Then, I'm going to tack another $1 an hour onto that." That meant I'd be making $8.90 an hour, which was a pretty big deal for a teenager back then.

I was on an upward trajectory.

CHAPTER 15

REVIVED
LOVE

That is my girl!

For the last year and a half, Ketty and I moved in the same circles. Her pastor invited me to speak at her church several times. Ketty was always there, and even though we gradually came to the point where we were both friendly to each other, that was where it stopped. There was absolutely nothing romantic between us.

Meanwhile, I still felt that she was the one for me. I tried hard to let go of my feelings for her, but just couldn't seem to do it. I wasn't pursuing her because I didn't want anyone or anything to distract me. I was focused. I often prayed about my feelings for Ketty as they were intensifying.

"God, you know I have these feelings for Ketty. Every time I see her, I like her even more. How do I deal with this? I don't want to be a disappointment to you and go after the wrong person. Help me understand if she's the right one."

God never answered me, at least not directly.

Every couple of weeks, I'd see a sign that would make me think she was, indeed, the right one. But I wasn't certain.

Just about the time I was wrapping up at Toys"R"Us, I told my friend Dan that I was looking for a job where I could work more hours. At Toys"R"Us, there was rarely room to breathe during the Christmas season, but after that, the place seemed like a ghost town. We were all scrambling to get hours. "If I could find another job during the week, I could work at Toys"R"Us on weekends," I told him.

The very next day, Dan called me and said he had heard about an internship at the Jersey City Housing Authority. He told me "You need to call a woman named Janet; she's expecting your call" and went on to give me her phone number.

The Curries Woods Coincidence

Within a week, I sat in Janet's office, interviewing for the job. I liked her immediately, as she seemed to be a kind woman with an easy laugh. The interview went well, and she told me that the recommendation was a huge point in my favor. I was elated when she hired me on the spot.

She said I'd be working in a brand-new facility in an area of Jersey City called Curries Woods. By this time, Ketty and I had become friends, so I called her and told her about my new internship, and added, "I'll be working in Curries Woods." I don't really know why I mentioned the part about "Curries Woods." It wasn't a particularly interesting detail.

As soon as she heard it, something seemed to happen on the other end of the line. I thought for a moment that the signal had dropped. Then, quietly, she asked, "Did you say 'Curries Woods'?"

"That's right. Why?"

"Did you know that I work for the Jersey City Housing Authority?"

I shook my head, "I had no idea."

"In Jersey City Heights."

"Okay." I wasn't sure where this was going.

"My boss told me yesterday that we're moving to a new office in Curries Woods."

I nearly dropped the phone. "Really? When is that going to happen?"

"Next week," she said.

As we continued to compare notes, we discovered we were going to be working in the same building, starting the same week. Coincidence? I didn't think so.

Side by Side

The day I reported to work, Janet was there to greet me with a big smile and take me into the main lobby, where there was a large desk, with two computers, two chairs and two stations.

"This is where you're going to be working," she told me. "Someone else will be sitting over here," she gestured toward the other chair, "but she works for another department."

It couldn't be, could it?

Yes, it could. About an hour later, Ketty arrived.

We were not only working in the same building, but at the same desk. We both had a laugh about it, but inside I was thanking God for His sense of humor.

Oh God, I need to be sure!

Still, I wasn't convinced, and my relationship with Ketty continued to be an important part of my prayers:

"God, that's pretty cool, but I'm not sure this was you. I need to know for sure that Ketty is the one."

As you know, I had grown up with a mother and father whose marriage was arranged by their parents, and that hadn't worked out too well for either one of them. As much as I loved Ketty, I wanted to make sure that when I got married, I was entering into a relationship certain that it was arranged by God.

Still, I think that as we worked together every day, she and I learned that we were alike in so many ways. She saw that my faith was real and that I was a person of integrity. I already knew that Ketty was a woman of faith but working alongside her made me even more sure about her good character. Working together was better than dating, because it allowed us to see each other in very real situations. We couldn't hide behind disguises and pretend we were better than we really were. We saw each other clearly.

A lot of single people make up a long list of the traits they want in a spouse, but there was only one item on my list: I wanted to marry a woman of faith who loved God. Period. She had to be pretty though, that was not negotiable.

Certainly, Ketty appeared to be the one for me. I also realized that there were countless of beautiful women who loved God. How can I be certain? I wasn't expecting that God would speak to me personally. I just wanted to hear more than that "still small voice" inside; I recalled how painful it was when Ketty broke up with me about four years prior. I am an all-in type of person, but I had to be 100 percent sure first.

In the meantime, my friend Larry from church decided to give politics a shot. He became one of eight people running for mayor of Jersey City. He didn't have any background in politics, nor any major endorsements or big money behind him. As an educator in the public school system, there were some important changes he wanted to see made in the city's politics, so he decided to throw his hat in the ring.

What happened next would become a very memorable time in my life.

Did God Speak?

One Saturday morning, Larry asked me and another gentleman from our church, Paul, to go campaign with him at the Newport Centre Mall—which is, ironically, where I first met Ketty by the movie theater—on the western bank of the Hudson, right across the river from lower Manhattan. We were all in the car, driving through Jersey City on our way to the mall. Larry was driving, I was in the front passenger seat, and Paul was sitting in the back. As we rode along, Larry was filling us in about all the things that were going on in Jersey City at the time, and what he was going to do if he became mayor.

We were about halfway to our destination when he suddenly stopped in mid-sentence, pointed at a church we were passing on Jersey Avenue and said to me, "I just want to tell you that there's a woman in there who God is preparing to be your wife." The sentence came completely out of nowhere. Then he went back to talking about politics.

I was in utter disbelief. He was pointing at Ketty's church, although he didn't know who she was.

"Wait a minute," I stopped him. "What did you just say?"

"About what?"

"You know. About God having a wife for me in that church?"

"Oh, nothing. I don't know. Really, I just felt that there's a girl in there that God is preparing for you."

I knew immediately that this was over the top. Maybe God had answered my prayer about Ketty in a way I could not doubt. Now it was time for me to stop praying and take action.

The following Saturday morning there was a prayer vigil at Ketty's church, and that's where I decided to give her the "good news"—at least it was good news for me—that she and I were going to wind up married someday.

After we finished praying, I told her, "Ketty, I've got to share something with you. I've been praying about this for a while now, and just a couple of days ago I got a crystal-clear answer. You are going to be my wife. And that's all I've got to say to you."

Well, she wasn't ready to hear it, and she stopped talking to me for four months. It was so awkward working with her. She was very respectful to me, but she had a different vision about who her husband was going to be.

During that time, I stayed faithful to my vision, but I didn't bother her or say anything more about it.

Several weekends later, I had heard Pastor Joshua tell us how he approached his wife before they were married. She took 11 months to respond to his request to date her. That story inspired me to wait. When it's something that good, it's worth the wait.

A New Year, a Bright Future

Then, on December 31, 2004, at my invitation Ketty attended a New Year's Eve service at my church. After the service was over, I sat in my car outside the church and called Ketty to make sure she had made it home safely.

We talked for about 10 minutes, and then she said, "By the way, Issa, do you remember how you told me that God spoke to you about me?"

"Of course, I do."

"Well, I just wanted to tell you that he showed me the same thing."

I put the phone on mute, punched my fist in the air and shouted, "Yes! Yes! Yes!"

Then I pushed the mute button again and resumed our conversation: "Okay! That's awesome! Wonderful! Now we're going to take it slow... but let's go out on our first date tonight."

And so our first official date was on New Year's Day of 2005.

CHAPTER 16

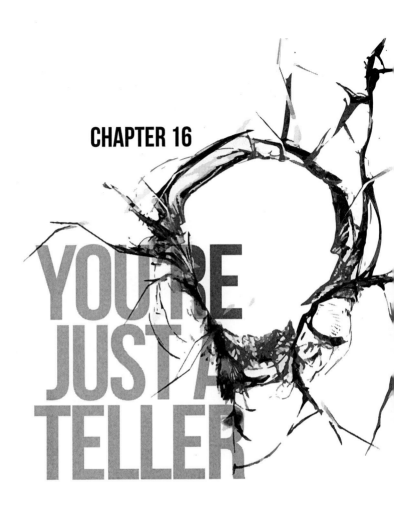

YOU'RE
JUST A
TELLER

My first business card

My career was about to take a sudden turn into an entirely new field—banking.

On a lazy afternoon, I walked into a Bank of America branch to make a small deposit. I struck up a conversation with the teller.

Just as I was turning to go, she asked me a question: "Have you ever thought about a career in banking?"

"No, not really. Why?"

"We're hiring tellers, and I was just thinking that you should apply."

I laughed. "That sounds good. Let me think about it."

My internship at the housing authority was coming to an end, but I didn't really want to be a teller. Nonetheless, the banking industry as a whole intrigued me, and I didn't want to pass up this opportunity to get my foot in the door. Maybe I could go into sales later on.

My goal was to sell banking products, just as I had sold the insurance policies at Toys"R"Us. I couldn't exactly sell them until I knew what they were. So, starting as a teller sounded like a very good deal to me. Plus, I would get health benefits, 401k plan, pension and a list of awesome benefits like 20 percent off of my cell phone bill.

More Than Just a Job

Within three weeks I was working as a teller at a branch in Jersey City's waterfront. I loved the Corporate America feel. The confidence I felt when wearing my suit and tie and walking into a business district was surreal. Although just a teller, I would look at high rises and feel like anything is possible.

Three months into my new job, I was transferred to a branch on 6th and Washington Street in Hoboken, a one square mile city that I loved from the start. I could tell right away that I had a different attitude about my job than most of my co-workers.

My immediate goal was to get into sales, so I asked my supervisor, Geneva, "What do I have to do to sell products?"

Immediately, she told me that I needed to learn all about credit cards. "I'm going to give you some information, and I want you to read it carefully. I want you to learn all about how credit cards work, and then you can start suggesting them to our customers."

I did as she asked, and it worked out pretty well. After wrapping my head around the product, I asked every customer if they would like to consider obtaining a Bank of America credit card. If I got a chance, I quickly explained why getting a credit card was such a good idea: It's convenient. It's easier than cash. It gives you a record of your expenditures. It's backed by one of the world's largest and most prestigious banks. And so on.

At the time, I was just 20 years old, and I was driving a car that was almost as old as I was. Every day, when I headed out on the 25-minute drive to Hoboken, I said a silent prayer that my old clunker would make it through one more day. When I did finally get that promotion, one of the first things I was going to do was buy a new car.

Six months into my new branch, Geneva made an announcement that caused my spirits to sink. She was being transferred to a branch in Jersey City. I had spent a lot of time trying to show her that I had what it takes to be a success in the banking industry—and now I was going to have to start all over with someone new.

Getting Off to a Bad Start

As it turned out, the new manager, Shiva, was instrumental in propelling me to the next level. Nonetheless, our relationship did not begin so well. One day, not too long after he had arrived, I got to work two minutes late. I was scheduled to start at 11 a.m., and I walked through the door at 11:02.

He was standing in the lobby when I walked in, and asked me in what I took to be a friendly tone, "Hey, can I talk to you for a minute?"

"Sure," I smiled.

"You're late."

I'm sure I looked surprised. That wasn't what I was expecting.

"I know," I said. "I'm sorry. I had trouble finding a parking space."

Being two minutes late wasn't really a big deal to me. But it was to him.

"Being late is not acceptable and it's inexcusable," he said. "And this is the last time you're going to be late. Do you understand that?"

"Yes, sir. Absolutely. It won't happen again."

Not a great way to get off to a start with the new boss. Now I felt like I was going to have to work twice as hard to show him that I wasn't a goof-off. To his credit, he didn't bring it up again. He had made his point and we both let it go. I was never late again.

About four weeks after our initial encounter over my tardiness, I finally got enough nerve to ask Shiva if I could meet with him. He took me into his office and closed the door. I took a deep breath and said, "Look, I love Bank of America. And I liked being a teller. But more than that, I love selling. You are the third manager I've had, and it's not fair."

He nodded, so I went on. "I had to prove myself to one manager, but before I could get myself situated, I got transferred here and had to prove myself to another manager who put me through a process of reading brochures. And now, boom, you come, and I have to repeat everything all over. I just want to sell."

"Well," he said, "here's what you have to do. If you want to be a salesperson, you have to start by being excellent at referring sales to the personal banker."

"How do I do that?"

"Refer five products every day. I don't care what they are." He ticked them off on his fingers. "Online banking, savings account, credit card account, a mortgage...When people come to you in the teller line, make it a point to notice if they're missing certain accounts, and if they are, refer them over to a personal banker. If you can do that, then I'll know you have what it takes to be a personal banker."

I smiled and said, "I got this!"

"Okay then, show me what you got."

Our conversation that day changed our relationship. From then on, in addition to my boss, he also took on the role of a mentor, watching what I was doing and giving me tips on how I could do it better.

Before I knew it, I was sending the personal banker an average of 5 products an hour, and Shiva was thrilled.

There was another man I noticed. Ironically, his name was Robert, and he reminded me so much of Robert De Niro, the famous actor. Robert was a mortgage lender who worked out of our branch a couple of times a month. He was a pleasant guy—an older gentleman about my dad's age—and I admired his focus and his work ethic. He was the type of person who stayed on-task all day long, going through his applications and returning his phone calls. He seemed to enjoy what he did, and I learned a lot from watching him work, and although I didn't know it, he was watching me too.

A few months later, Shiva called me into his office and gave me some news that was good for him, but not so great for me. He was being promoted, and that meant he was leaving the Hoboken branch. I was shocked, of course, and wondered if that meant I'd have to start over, yet again—even after I'd worked so hard to show what I could do.

It turned out that he was leaving that very afternoon, and I asked him if I could give him a lift to his new location.

"That would be great," he replied.

As I helped him carry his things out to my car, I suddenly wished that I hadn't offered to give him a ride. I hadn't thought about the fact that my car was—to put it politely—a piece of junk. I was embarrassed for him to see it, much less ride in it.

As soon as we got to my car, I started apologizing about it. I told him that someday, I'd be driving a better car. "All I need is an opportunity."

The boss laughed. "I'm going to give you that opportunity," he said.

"What do you mean?"

"Effective immediately, you're getting a salary increase to the next position, which is a sales and service specialist." He explained that I'd still be working as a teller half of the time I was in the bank, but the other half, I would be functioning as a salesperson. "This is a perfect way for you to make the transition into being a personal banker." He went on to tell me that my starting salary in this new position would be $28,000 a year. At that age, it sounded like a whopping amount of money!

I was so happy that day, within two or three weeks, I was transferred to a branch on Second and Hudson in Hoboken. I no longer had to tell my friends that I was a teller. I became a banker. I took learning about Bank of America seriously. I wanted to know every reason why we were America's leading bank. I became a fount of knowledge. I wanted customers to know they could trust us because that made them more likely to want to partner with us. Things were going well; I was on my way!

Maybe it was time to take my relationship with Ketty to the next level. I am Mr. Banker now!

CHAPTER 17

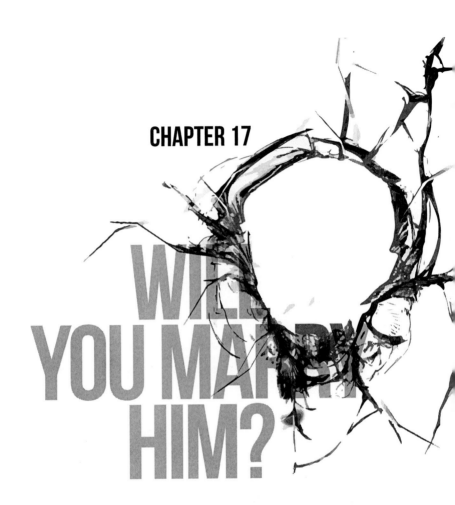

WILL YOU MARRY HIM?

She is hot!

Now that my career was on the upswing, I felt I could do something I'd wanted to do for a long, long time. I could ask Ketty to marry me.

The first thing I had to do was inform Ketty's parents and older brother Victor that I was going to propose to her. They were delighted, much to my relief.

I immediately started planning my proposal. It had to be done just right.

Of course, I wanted to give Ketty the most beautiful ring I could find, which was only fitting for the world's most beautiful girl. Fortunately, I had a cousin in California who worked in the diamond business, so I called and asked him to help me find a ring with a princess-cut diamond. He came through with a gorgeous piece of jewelry. The diamond was absolutely dazzling! There was only one problem. It was way more expensive than I could afford.

"Don't worry about it," my cousin said. "I'll buy it and you can pay me back in installments."

Everybody needs a cousin like that!

I wanted to propose to Ketty on her birthday so it wouldn't be so obvious. I decided to take her to one of her favorite restaurants, the Brownstone Diner. I invited both of our families and some friends to come. I let them know that they had to be there because I was going to propose to Ketty and elicited a promise to keep it a secret.

Now, Ketty comes from a big family—she has two brothers and two sisters—and my family is a big one as well, so there were twenty of us sitting around the table that early evening.

We enjoyed a delicious dinner, and then I suggested that we should go around the table and tell Ketty how much she meant to us. I arranged it so I would be the last one to share.

You should have heard the beautiful things people had to say about my wonderful future wife. No one needed any prompting to say great things about her. A huge lump formed in my throat as I heard all their heartfelt comments and agreed with every one of them.

Finally, it was my turn to talk.

Instead, I said, "Ketty, turn around. There's someone here who has a question for you."

She turned and saw that a waiter had quietly come up behind her. He was carrying a tray of flowers, with an engagement ring in the center, and was wearing a t-shirt that I had hand-lettered, which said: "Will you marry him?"

When she turned back around, she saw that I was down on one knee.

"Ketty," I said, "I love you. And in the presence of your family and mine, I want to know the answer to this man's question."

She was baffled briefly before bursting into tears—and I almost did the same. Then she took the ring out of the flowers, slipped it onto her finger and shouted, "Yes!"

Our families burst into cheers and applause as we kissed.

Ketty and I were engaged!

The $40,000 Bombshell

It wasn't until a few weeks after that big night that Ketty's parents hit me with a bombshell.

I was talking to them about how much I loved their daughter, and how I couldn't wait to be married to her, when they said, "It's great that you're engaged. But of course, you can't get married for a while."

"Pardon me?" I wasn't sure what was going on.

"You can't get married until you're making at least $40,000 a year,"

I didn't say it, but I was thinking, "$40,000? That's a lot of money!" It was, especially for those days. I wasn't making anywhere near $40,000 a year.

They went on to explain, "That's how much it takes to provide for a family. And that's just for the two of you."

Learning More About Ketty's Parents

As I talked further with Ketty's parents that day, they told me something I didn't know. Just as my family had come to the United States from Jordan, Ketty's family had emigrated from Ecuador. Her dad was a retired Seiko watchmaker who had worked hard to build a life for his family in their new country. Her mother was self-employed in the jewelry business. While the journey to establish themselves in America may have been challenging enough, one can only imagine how resilient they were while raising five children along the way.

They loved Ketty and wanted her to be financially secure.

As I left their house that day, I was already calculating how I was going to boost my salary to $40,000 as quickly as possible.

I know now that my desire to marry Ketty made a big difference in my career. It gave me the fuel I needed to work hard and to fight for the promotions I deserved.

Any life coach will tell you that setting goals is an essential key to success. I had a terrific goal. I wanted to get married!

CHAPTER 18

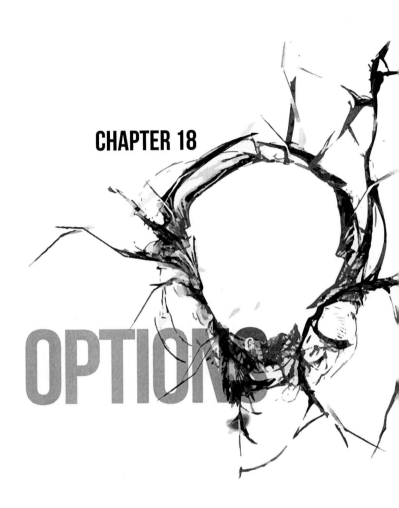

OPTIONS

Commitment

Now that Ketty and I were officially engaged, I felt like I was walking on air. I know that's an old cliché, but I can't think of a better way to describe the joy I felt. Every once in a while, during the middle of an ordinary day, I would remember, "Ketty said yes! She's going to be my wife. What did I do to deserve this?" and a thrill would surge through me.

I had no idea that I was standing at a crossroads and was about to be faced with a decision that would have a profound impact on my career.

We had run out of deposit slips, and I volunteered to run back to the branch where I used to work on 6th Street to pick some up.

It just so happened that Robert, the mortgage guy was there, and he seemed pleased to see me.

"Issa! Where have you been?"

I explained that I had been promoted and had been transferred to a different branch.

"That's really great! Good for you!" He lowered his voice just a bit. "But listen, I've actually been wanting to talk to you."

"You have?"

"I'm looking for a junior loan officer. In fact, I need two. One for Hudson County and one for Bergen County. I think you'd be perfect for one of those positions. Would you consider joining my team?"

"Oh my gosh," I said. "It sounds great! But I just got promoted six months ago and I really want to be in sales."

"I understand that," he said. "But, Issa, this is sales. You really ought to get involved in the mortgage side of things. It's so lucrative—and you'd be great at it."

He went on to explain that if I did as he wanted me to do, I would no longer receive a salary, but rather, my income would be based entirely on commission. The bank would give me a $2,000 monthly draw. If I didn't make that much in commissions, that would cover my expenses and the bank will take it back later. The amount I "owed" would be deducted from the commission from my loan closings. If my commissions totaled more than $2,000 and I did not have a balance, I would keep the entire amount.

The way Robert talked, making $2,000 in commissions was a snap, and I'd probably make much more. Still, it was a big risk for a young guy just starting out in the business.

I didn't know what to do. I had just received a promotion that I had been waiting for. I certainly didn't want to seem ungrateful to Shiva, who had shown such faith in me.

I hemmed and hawed for a bit, and then finally asked Robert to give me his card and said I'd be sure to keep in touch with him. He may have thought I was just trying to put him off, but I was intrigued. The more I thought about the move, the more I liked it. So after another three months, I called him and asked if his offer was still open. I was thrilled when he told me it was.

I told him I had discovered that nobody in the branch really understood the ins and outs of the mortgage business. They understood that a mortgage was a loan to be paid back on a monthly basis, but that was about all. I understood there was much more to it, and I wanted to learn everything I could. There is no such thing as too much knowledge. Everything you know provides one more way you can build a successful career.

After much contemplation, I left the Bank's retail banking to go work for its mortgage department. When I told Shiva what I was doing, he was not happy.

"Issa, you're making a mistake," he said. "The mortgage industry is about to have a crisis and you don't want to be there. A lot of people are going to lose their jobs..."

He was absolutely right about that, but he backed off when I told him I had made a commitment and that I was really interested in learning everything I possibly could about mortgages.

The first few months were difficult. I was learning a lot, but I wasn't closing many deals, so my income was less than it would have been if I had just stayed put on the retail side of the business.

Another complication, as far as I was concerned, was that I was still not making anywhere near that $40,000 annual salary that I needed in order to marry Ketty. Still, I was learning everything I could, and making contacts that I believed would benefit me in the long run. I had learned that taking big risks can bring big rewards and that risk, in fact, is a necessary component of success. If anyone has any doubts about it, taking risks or leaps is not the same thing as cutting corners or making shady deals. Integrity is vital in all walks of life.

Finally, six months into my new career, I began to get some traction and started to close deals. Things were looking up and our wedding day was getting closer.

Have I Got an Offer for You!

Things took an unexpected turn for me when I noticed an email from Shiva that came in precisely at midnight. He was now a Consumer Market Manager, overseeing the operation of a cluster of branches in Northern New Jersey.

"Issa give me a call. I have a position for you as a personal banker—something you've always wanted."

He was right. He was offering something I had always wanted. Six months ago, I would have been jumping up and down with joy. For now, I felt torn, because I owed so much to Robert. He had become something of a father figure, and I didn't want to let him down.

It was a tempting offer, especially when Shiva told me that I would be given a starting salary of $34,000 a year, with the potential of earning up to $4,000 per quarter in bonuses. Even if I only made an extra $1,500 a quarter, that would bring my salary to $40,000 a year. That would be enough to marry Ketty—and that was what I wanted most in life.

So, after getting the job offer to become a personal banker, I called Robert and asked for advice. I knew I could trust him to tell me exactly what he thought I should do. He was the type of mentor every young person needs. Robert wasn't happy because he hated to lose me, especially after investing so much time in me. Yet, he knew it was the best decision for me and said, "Why don't you go for it?"

And so, I called Shiva and accepted his offer. This was a very bittersweet time for me. All of a sudden, I felt more prepared for marriage than ever. At this time, I called Ketty to tell her about my new promotion and salary increase. I also told her to share the news with her parents so we could begin wedding plans. What an exciting time! I always kept my pastor abreast of my career development, so I informed him of my new role.

Personal Growth

It was the end of 2007, five years into my new walk of faith and to my surprise, my pastor invited me to be ordained as a deacon/minister at the church. "Say what?" I know, that's exactly what I thought at first. Yet I felt honored, humbled, and nervous to say the least. The pastor was expanding and reorganizing the leadership team for the next level of growth. Thanks to Pastor Paula, who led a 40 Days of Purpose Campaign, the ministry began growing rapidly. It must have grown from serving at least 250 families in 2002 to over 350 families in 2007. With growth came the workload. The weddings, hospital visits, funerals and general needs of the parishioners had nearly tripled.

As a 22 year old, this represented an important highlight in my spiritual journey. I recall being the youngest candidate for such serious consideration. Almost immediately after my ordination as minister, the pastor wasted no time. He called me to ask if I would lead the video and sound ministries, which had a substantial number of volunteers. I was not expecting that, so I froze.

"I know you don't have experience in this area, but I am confident that you'll do well, son. You don't need the technical skills, but rather the people and leadership skills." He uttered.

As a young man with an open heart to serve, I did not realize that these service opportunities in church were preparing me for greater things down the road.

Trouble on the Horizon

The truth was that I had seen some things in the mortgage industry that had me worried. I knew that when a bank gave out a loan, it needed to be sure that the borrower intended to pay it back, and that he or she also had the capability of paying it back. It seemed to me at the time that some people were being approved for loans that they could never hope to repay. If we declined a loan and another bank easily approved it, that didn't make much sense to me. Sooner or later, this whole system was going to come tumbling down.

As you may remember, late in 2008, Bank of America paid over $2 billion to acquire Countrywide Financial, a mortgage company based in California. When Countrywide was acquired, Bank of

America also took on billions of dollars' worth of loans that had not originated according to sound banking principles. Over the next five-plus years, Bank of America absorbed an estimated $50 billion in losses. Warning bells were sounding. It was not the best time to be in the mortgage business.

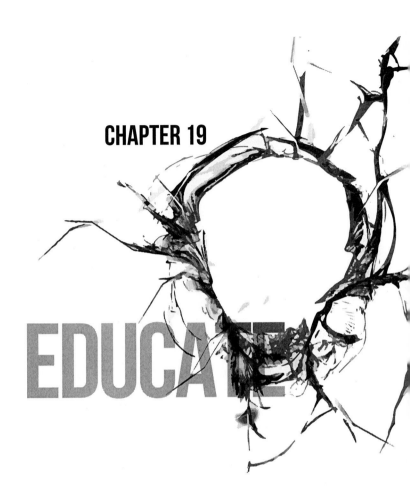

CHAPTER 19

EDUCATE

That same year, I started working in a branch in Lodi, NJ as a personal banker. I had a terrific new manager, Cathy, who possessed many years of banking experience. She was impressed with my experience and fostered an atmosphere for good performance. I did not feel like I had to prove myself I knew I was qualified for the job. She instantly recognized my potential and did everything she could to nurture it.

Now, most of the personal bankers were not trained to write mortgages. Rather, if someone wanted to buy a new home or refinance an existing mortgage, they would be sent to someone who specialized in mortgages. Personal bankers felt that mortgages were complex and mysterious, and they could only be processed by people with years of special training. While most personal bankers were almost afraid of mortgages, I leveraged my experience and took them on.

This meant, among other things, that I was bringing in more loans, so my bonuses were higher, and Cathy loved it. In fact, because of my mortgage experience, I was exceeding my lending goals by 700 to 800 percent. Sometimes I would hit as high as 1100 percent of the goal. This also meant that Cathy's overall performance goals would be met easily, practically guaranteeing her bonuses.

It was such a pleasure for me to sit down with people and help them get their finances under control. It often went something like this:

"Okay, you're paying $3,000 a month on your mortgage, $400 on your car and another $900 on your personal loans and credit cards. That's over $4300 a month. Why don't we do this? Let's refinance your home at the current interest rate, which is much lower than what you have. We'll pay off your car and your credit cards—and you'll wind up with one monthly payment that's more than $1200 less than you're paying right now."

"Can I really do that?"

"Of course, you can."

I was surprised to find that many people were literally throwing thousands of dollars away, simply because they didn't know the financial possibilities that were open to them.

Now I know that some people hate the banks. They blame bankers for most of, if not all, the evil things that are happening in the world today. And, of course, we've seen how some banks and bankers have gotten off-track and have allowed greed to get them involved in all kinds of shenanigans.

A good, honest, competent banker can be a godsend to ordinary families everywhere. Proper financial guidance can help people achieve success in life. It can enable them to build a secure future for themselves and their children.

So Many Opportunities to Help

Do you remember George Bailey, the character played by James Stewart in the movie, *It's a Wonderful Life*? I know, my mother wasn't even born when the movie came out. But that's a banker for you! He saved his entire community. It may seem corny, but I believe he represents the kind of hero an honest banker can be.

I was amazed by the many opportunities I discovered to help people achieve a better life.

After several quarters at the Lodi Bank of America, I got a phone call from the manager of the branch in Fort Lee. I was excited to take that call because the Fort Lee branch was always a top performer.

"Issa," he said, "I'm looking at all of your numbers, and I see that you're doing fantastic, especially concerning mortgages."

"Thank you very much."

"I'm calling because I have a meeting with my staff on Saturday morning at eight o'clock, and I wonder if you'd be able to come in and talk to them about mortgages and share your success."

"Sure, but let me check with Cathy" I said. "By the way, who do you want me to talk to?" I asked.

"Everyone. My tellers, service associates, the assistant manager, all my personal bankers—everyone. Don't worry Issa, I already cleared it with Cathy."

"Great, how about if I take the first twenty minutes or so to talk specifically to the tellers about how to keep their eyes open for mortgage opportunities. This way they can feel confident referring mortgage needs to personal bankers. After that, I'll spend some time talking to the personal bankers about how to handle the referrals they get from the tellers—what to say, how to say it, and so forth."

I came and presented to the entire group for about 45 minutes. I had only covered a fraction of the material I wanted to share. The tellers had to get to their stations because the bank was scheduled to open for business in a few minutes.

I still had to talk to the personal bankers, so we went into a private office.

After my presentation was finally over, the bank manager came over to talk to me. He had a well-dressed, important-looking woman with him, but I had no idea who she was. Before I had a chance to introduce myself to her, she said, "Hi, my name is Jaime, and we need to find a way to leverage you much better. How did you learn so much about mortgages in particular?"

It turned out that she was the consumer market executive for our region. In other words, she was the big boss lady. She went on to say, "What you did today—I want you to do it for all the managers, all the assistant managers, all the personal bankers and all the sales associates. I want you to train everyone in our region."

I was thrilled! I loved sharing my knowledge with other people, equipping them to be even better at what they did. It was nerve-racking, knowing that I was going to be training all the managers. I kept thinking, what did I do to deserve this? I am still just this immigrant boy from Jordan with a dream.

Over the next several months, I conducted several seminars for bank employees at the corporate offices in Teaneck, NJ. Bear in mind that I was in my early 20s, and some of the people I was training were in their 40s and 50s. Many of them had been with Bank of America for decades. Any trepidation that I felt was quickly erased by the way they listened to me and seemed to appreciate what I had to tell them. That was a fun time for me.

Now, it was during all of this that Bank of America got into trouble because of its purchase of Countrywide Mortgage. For several quarters in a row, the bank posted big losses. There was speculation in the media that the entire company was at risk of going bankrupt.

At this point, Ketty and I had contracted a long list of vendors to accommodate our wedding, scheduled in the coming months. I took the bad news to every vendor, reminding them that I was a banker and that I was getting worried about the economy. I offered many of them an immediate payment in full in exchange for reduced rates. Most vendors agreed, and we saved a substantial amount of money.

Citizenship

Over the last several months before our wedding, I had been thinking more and more about becoming an American citizen. The thought filled me with excitement, but there was always so much to do, and I just couldn't seem to get around to it.

When Ketty and I were planning our honeymoon trip overseas, I suddenly realized I'd need a passport. Furthermore, I couldn't get a passport unless I was a U.S. citizen.

That was the end of my procrastination, and I took an important step that I am so very proud of. After eleven years as a permanent resident, I became a United States citizen.

I had goosebumps on the day I took the Oath of Citizenship, surrounded by other men and women from countries around the world who had chosen to make America their home. I still get goosebumps when I think of it today!

This was such a great moment in my life, and to top it all off, Ketty and I were finally getting married.

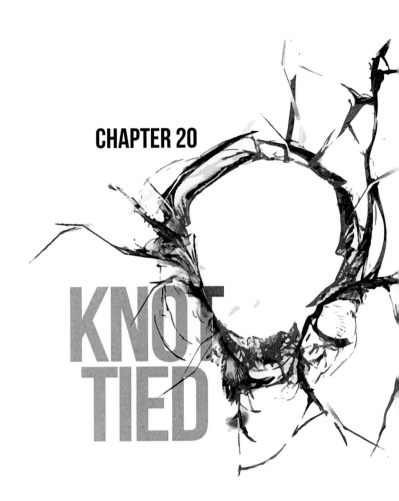

CHAPTER 20

KNOT
TIED

love

Like most people, I've had many happy days in my life.

The day my mom came to take me and my brothers from Theodor Schneller school in 1998 ranks very high on my list.

So does the day we boarded an airplane headed for the United States and the day I wore that black shirt at Toys"R"Us. Needless to say, the time I reconnected with my faith is unforgettable.

Not one of those happy events matches the absolute joy I felt on May 30, 2009, the day I married Ketty, the absolute love of my life.

The skies were clear, and the weather was warm with a calming breeze. It seemed like nature was celebrating with us. There was only one dark cloud, and that was that I wished my biological father could had come from Jordan to join us. I hadn't seen him in eleven years, but I wanted him to be there to celebrate with me on my wedding day. There I was, at the church early, and I kept thinking about my dad. Although I was prepared to cover his travel expenses, he had reasons to stay. His words echoed in my head while I was pacing on stage. "The airplane ticket is expensive. There are more important ways to use that money." I know he never meant those words the way they came out. I brushed it off, thinking that maybe he's dealing with his own insecurities and did not want to be near my stepdad—I completely got it.

When I looked up, my stepfather was there with a happy smile on his face. I wish I could say that the barriers I've built in my heart concerning my stepfather vanished that day. They remained neutral. I was about to get married, but the little boy inside of me was yearning to see dad, but other than my father not being there, the day was perfect.

Ketty and I were married and celebrated in front of 200+ friends and family members onboard a boat in New York Harbor. What I remember most about that day was that Ketty was a vision of loveliness in her gorgeous ivory dress. The off-the-shoulder gown was elegantly decorated with pearls and had a tufted cathedral-length bustle train, which trailed gracefully behind her.

My brothers Jacob and Hanna, looking razor-sharp, served as my co-best men, and Ketty's sisters, Vicky and Laura, dressed in stunning teal gowns, were the Maids of Honor. All of Ketty's siblings and nearly all of mine were part of our wedding party. We were 20-strong on that beautifully decorated stage. The bridesmaids carried exquisitely arranged and radiantly lit lanterns as they stood on stage in their fuchsia gowns.

We were delighted to have Pastor Joshua Rodriguez, who had meant so much to me over the years, perform the ceremony. Ketty's pastor, Pastor Pedro Cabrera, also took part, presiding over Holy Communion.

The boat's glass-paneled walls provided breath-taking views of the New York City skyline and the Statue of Liberty.

I was so proud, excited and happy as I pledged to take Ketty as my wife, and as I heard her profess her love for me. It had been a long, bumpy road to the altar for us, but now I felt that all my dreams were coming true.

Our reception also featured a classy and delicious cake, prepared by Buddy Valastro of Carlo's Bakery in Hoboken. We didn't know it at the time, but two weeks before our wedding, Buddy, the baker released his first TV episode of his new show *Cake Boss*. Shortly after, he became one of the best-known bakers in the United States. Today, *Cake Boss* remains one of the most popular cooking shows on TV.

Before we knew it, our wonderful day was over, and Ketty and I were on our way to an unforgettable ten-day honeymoon on the beautiful island of Puerto Rico.

Television?

The happiness of marriage overflowed to my career. Bank of America was financially strong despite the Countrywide debacle, but it was taking a beating in the media, and something had to be done to restore the bank's public image.

Ultimately, corporate executives decided to put together a national advertising campaign—The Financial Wellbeing Campaign—to tell the bank's story. They felt the urgency to explain that even though there had been some turbulent times recently, the overall financial position of the bank was extremely strong.

The bank's regional executives were each asked to find three or four employees who could tell the story of Bank of America by sharing their own stories—what they liked about their jobs, what they considered to be the bank's strengths, and so forth.

Our Market Executive, Jaime, invited me to apply. I was driven into New York City, where I auditioned in front of a number of bank executives, as well as the producer and his team. Of course, I had spent a lot of time learning about what made Bank of America so special, and I had all those facts and figures at my fingertips. Plus, I truly loved my job.

I guess my enthusiasm showed, because I got the part and appeared in two commercials that were shown on national TV in 2009.

When the commercials aired, a few noticed. Besides Bank of America associates, a friend said he looked in the window of a bar and grill and saw me in the TV screen. He said, "I couldn't believe it! How did you get to be on TV?"

For the most part, as public as this win was, it felt private. Yet it was wins like these and others that weren't celebrated so much that placed a smile in my heart. It kept me wondering. Is there more?

CHAPTER 21

LAUNDRY

Sophia Isabella Musharbash

After the commercial aired, a position opened up for a Business Specialist in my banking center, which is like being a personal banker, but for business owners. Cathy recommended me for the role, and I quickly got the promotion. "Wow, more responsibility, more money. How far do I want to move up?" Seven months into my new role, I realized that my career advancement had been tied to a larger goal. It was about producing sufficient income to marry Ketty. Since I'd accomplished this, I needed a new and bigger goal. So, I began searching for another challenge, this time with my wife. I desperately needed wisdom to guide me forward.

Ten months into our marriage, in March 2010 Ketty and I welcomed our firstborn, Sophia. Her name means wisdom, and she was exactly what we needed. Becoming a father was very important to me. I was so looking forward to it. I had seen good examples of fatherhood that I wanted to emulate. I've also seen many fatherless children. I knew that the damage caused by absent paternity is seemingly beyond repair.

I knew what this responsibility entailed and was so eager to take my place as a father.

Bank of America offered three months of paternity leave, and I took it in its entirety. Many things were going on in my life, and I felt it was time to take stock and think about where I wanted to go and ultimately what I wanted to do. Ketty and I couldn't travel for our first wedding anniversary, because Sophia was too young. So we celebrated in our apartment, missing the beauty of sandy beaches.

I was approaching my 25th birthday, which sounds young until you think about the fact that it's a quarter of a century. I was married to the love of my life. We had just had a beautiful baby girl and had just purchased our first property, a two-family home. Looking back at all the challenges and victories, I felt that I was prepared for my next level, especially with this amazing partner, Ketty.

Ketty and I both knew we wanted more children. I had to be sure that every step I took was the right one for my growing family. Of course, I wanted to take care of them financially. I also wanted to be able to spend time with them. I started to desire a more flexible work schedule. I didn't want to miss important occasions like birthdays and school programs because I was stuck at the office.

I liked the idea of going into real estate, especially after going through the purchase of our first home. I felt like I already knew the ins and outs of the mortgage business, which I thoroughly enjoyed. If I started my own real estate firm, I figured I would gain the freedom to build a business around my family life. I knew I'd have to work hard, and I was fine with that. I had done it all my life.

So, before that three-month paternity leave was over, I enrolled in a two-week real estate course and got my pre-licensing certificate. Next, I had to take a state exam. I studied hard in the week leading up to the exam and passed on my first try. The search for a brokerage began. I wanted to work for a big brand, like Bank of America, yet stay as close to home as possible to be near Sophia. So, I found an office with a recognized franchise in my town and asked for an interview that turned into an on-the-spot offer. I made the mistake of not interviewing three firms and see what other offers would look like. I figured I could stay close to home and begin my real estate career by working part time on nights and weekends.

I went back to work at the bank as I was awaiting state licensing, but it was never the same. Real estate had captured my attention and I wanted to learn more. Ketty noticed immediately, but kept it to herself at first.

On one early morning, Ketty woke up and turned to me as I was still asleep. Caressing my face with her gentle hands, she said, "Issa, you need to pursue your real estate dreams. Go all the way and do it full-time. I have seen you thrive in so many situations. You can do this."

A part of her wanted me to recover my zeal and zest. She wanted to see the hunger again, and knew I needed this. She also knew that I was worried by the possibility that we could lose all the benefits provided by corporate America. With new responsibilities as parents and homeowners, it felt like a huge gamble. Ketty insisted, "If you want to leave the bank and go into real estate full time, you have my full support."

As I wiped the sleep from my eyes, I thought, I'd better jump on this quickly before Ketty changes her mind. I opened my eyes and looked at her with a new confidence and said, "Okay love, let's do this."

Goodbye to Banking

That morning, I wrote my resignation letter and gave my boss 30 days' notice. I wanted to show respect to the company that gave me so many opportunities to learn and grow. I explained to my boss my next move. She thought it was risky for this season of my life but knew that I'd had substantial time off to think it through. She did not try to change my mind, and gently said, "Be cautious, Issa. That consistent paycheck is not guaranteed out there." I smiled and said, "Thank you for everything, Cathy. It was an amazing journey with you."

I told my wife that for the first 90 days, I would be working a rigorous schedule, from 9 a.m. to 9 p.m., Monday through Saturday and a few hours after church on Sundays. I knew she would be with Sophia for a long time without me. My mother babysat when Ketty worked in the morning, and Ketty had the baby all by herself after work. I promised her, "At night, don't you worry about waking up for Sophia. I'll handle the night shift until she begins sleeping through the night." I felt the need to give more of myself at home, sensing what would come ahead. We needed to prepare for this adjustment in our schedule because I needed to have a better learning curve than the average new agent. I'm happy to have kept that promise for years, not only to stay up for Sophia, but our second born, Abraham as well.

Up hill battle

I'd like to tell you that my new career in real estate was an immediate success, and I became an overnight millionaire. But if I said that, I'd be lying. The truth is, we went through some very tough times.

Ninety days turned into five months. I couldn't quickly figure out a way to bring a steady flow of income into my household and replace my former salary. It didn't help that I earned 42 percent of the commissions from my sales and rentals, and then had to share 50 percent of it with a senior agent assigned to supervise my first six transactions. When my first rental listing brought me $84 before tax, I knew something wasn't right.

We tapped into our emergency savings and whatever we'd accumulated in our retirement funds just to keep our heads above water.

What I thought was a well-organized industry turned out to be an "every man for himself" type of career. There was no consistent training, coaching, administrative support, marketing or technology provided. You had to figure it all out, alone and at your own expense. Furthermore, everyone in your office was your competitor, including your boss, the broker.

In those first five tough months, I earned $5,500 from my real estate work. Most of this came from my first closing, which came to me because my brother in-law Victor and his wife Giselle needed to buy a home. I also processed a small number of rental transactions.

One thing I enjoyed was working on short sales on behalf of other agents. This allowed me to leverage my banking background pretty well. I could not go into the new year, 2011, with such instability in my income. I had worked hard since the age of 12 and now I was considering going back into banking again.

During this time, I was speaking to many homeowners who were behind on their mortgage payments for months and yet wanted to avoid foreclosure. Many came as referrals from lenders, attorneys and friends. Others came from seminars and community events where I spoke on the topic of short sales as an alternative to foreclosure. I would spend time explaining The Mortgage Forgiveness Relief Act of 2007. It essentially waived tax liability associated with mortgage debt forgiveness to those who qualified. Of course, I advised everyone to consult a tax professional before making any decisions, but for many, it was clearly the best thing to do.

Many of the families I talked to had endured devastating hardships. Their home values dropped well below their mortgage balance. Some lost their primary source of income and couldn't afford to pay their mortgage. Since their mortgage balance was higher than the property's value, they couldn't sell either. They were trapped. I'd spent time educating them on the short-sale process and dealing with their lenders. Some lenders offered financial assistance to sellers to offload these loans from their portfolios.

I kept my eyes on the prize. I took out buyers and presented offers. I negotiated short sales and listed homes for sale and apartments for rent. I was running around like a mad man, and short sales began to materialize. Still, I knew it was not going to be enough.

To be completely honest, I was having trouble making my own mortgage payment. It was embarrassing to think that even though I was going around telling people how to get out from under crushing debt and teaching them how to take advantage of a short sale—I was getting further behind and deeper in debt every month.

Because I was struggling to pay our mortgage, I eventually fell two-weeks behind. That wasn't good, but it fell within the 15-day grace period, so it wasn't horrible. Then I fell another two weeks behind, so now I was a full month late. Here I am with a strong background in finance, knowing all the ins and outs of mortgages, and yet I was about to lose my home because I had made the transition into full time real estate. I was in a constant cycle of trying to keep up.

It was a terrifying time in my life, but it did one good thing for me, it gave me empathy for people.

Meanwhile, my broker was busy doing commercial real estate, managing property and was privately working on moving our office to another location. Our entire company was kept in the dark.

Working in the Laundromat

One morning we were asked to report to another location, which was a functioning laundromat.

"Guys," we were told, "If you give me some time, what looks like a laundromat will become a top producing real estate office, just be patient with me."

I understood and stayed put for a while.

I remember having a client who placed an offer on a distressed property for $80,000. When he came to the office to sign the contract, he brought $80,000 in cash. Now that is very unusual, but I continued with the transaction. There was nothing in our policy that stopped someone from bringing in cash to purchase a home. He had all the money wrapped neatly but carried in a plastic bag, so it wasn't so obvious walking in the street. Amanda, who was the office administrator told me to take the client to the back of the office and she would help me count. We counted every last bill, all while the machines were washing and drying in the background. The lighting was dim, the walls were distressed. The place was pretty quiet. All we heard was the sound of the machines spinning and us counting. It felt like some crazy drug deal out of a movie.

I respected my broker because we all have a process in life. This was a critical time in my transition and my family depended on me.

I asked to meet with him to discuss going back to banking.

"Benjamin, I can't continue working like this, I have a wife and daughter and a mortgage, and I've depleted all of my savings. I'm going back to banking."

"I understand. You have to do what's best for your family." That was all the encouragement I got.

I told him, "But before I do that, I want to try another office in Hoboken. I will give it 60 days and if it doesn't pan out, it's back to banking."

He shook his head. "Issa, if you can't make it here, you won't make it anywhere. So many new agents think Hoboken is better because home prices are higher."

"I know that," I protested. "But that's not why I'm going there."

"What agents don't realize is that the competition is so big for that little town," he said. "You're better off staying here a little longer, or selling real estate part time and going back to banking."

I couldn't delay anymore, so I respectfully resigned, left behind a number of incomplete transactions, and joined the Hoboken office of the same franchise on January 2, 2011.

CHAPTER 22

FOCUSED

Sophia's 1st Birthday!

What a difference!

When I took a job at the Hoboken office, I quickly realized that each real estate office runs differently—Even if it's the same franchise. They may share a logo and website, but the day-to-day management is up to the franchisee.

The new office was professionally designed, with an open concept and had sufficient support staff. The broker was not competing with her own agents. Most brokers would take all the good leads for themselves and offer their agents the leftovers. This office was different. To top it off, I got a decent raise to my commission split and even the franchise fee was lower. That was a bit strange, since my prior office was charging more for the same franchise.

I attended my first office/sales meeting at the end of January and immediately fell in love with the place when Jessica, my new broker, announced the winner of January's rental competition.

"Congrats to Eric on another big win!"

We cheered and applauded Eric as Jessica handed him the Dunkin' Donuts gift card. She then announced a listing competition for the month of February, and that just lit me up.

She said, "Whoever brings in the most listings will be February's winner."

All the sensations I had felt at Toys"R"Us during my black shirt pursuit flared up. I was so new, but I wanted to win. I forgot what the prize was for February, but it didn't matter. I needed to make a name for myself in this new territory. I pumped myself up and got right to work. Nothing distracted me it was as if all the worries of the world came to a halt as I began pushing through for this competition.

Every day, I picked up the local newspaper and brought it to my office. I would turn to the real estate section and look at ads from landlords trying to lease their apartments. I knew that listing homes for sale was my goal, but landlords needed help too. Plus, rental listings had little to no competition. Most agents felt like rentals were a waste of time, required too much work and did not pay enough. I felt the opposite.

I realized that today's landlords are tomorrow's sellers and buyers. I figured, "If I can service them now with their current rental needs, they'll remember me when it's time to buy or sell." So, I hammered that phone, one landlord after the other. The conversations I had went like this:

"Good morning, my name is Issa Musharbash, I'm a real estate agent calling about your apartment for rent. I just saw it in the paper. Is it still available?"

"Yes, it is. But I don't really work with agents."

"I see, that's not a problem. I just thought I'd give you a call since your ad says that your apartment is newly renovated, and I am working with tenants that need immediate occupancy. Many landlords tell me their units are renovated, but when I get there it's a different story. Look, if you change your mind, please give me a call."

"Wait a second, I renovated this apartment, and it is immaculate. Did you say you're working with tenants?"

"Yes, every single day. I'm sorry sir, I didn't get your name?"

"My name is Marco. Hey, look, why don't you bring your tenants to my apartment, it's impressive. I just don't want to sign anything."

"No worries Marco, we can discuss that when I see the apartment. I am so glad you take pride in your property. I am honestly tired of seeing neglected apartments priced so high. So, before I take anyone there, I've got to see it in person."

"Come now and see for yourself. The floors are brand-new. The kitchen has cherry cabinets with black countertops and stainless-steel appliances. I put a lot of money into this unit. I'm sorry, what's your name again?"

"My name is Issa; I am looking forward to meeting you. Is 2 p.m. ok?

"Issa? That's a nice name. But I want you to know I am not signing any agreements."

"Thank you, Marco, and I understand. Let's first see if your apartment qualifies. Everything else will be addressed when I see you".

"Ok. I'll be waiting."

I knew objections would come, one after the other, but I also knew the purpose of my calls. I just wanted an appointment. I did not want to discuss commissions, signatures, or their other valid concerns over the phone. These concerns were just another way of saying, "I don't know you yet." I knew I could handle every concern in person when the prospective client got to see me and know me a bit more. For now, the most important thing was to get an appointment to view the apartment.

I eventually met Marco and began leasing all of his vacant units. He was particularly impressed with my ability to lease his units quickly, to qualified families and, most of the time, before construction was completed. He went on to refer me to other landlords in town like Tony and Christine. If I couldn't get a landlord on the phone, I would leave a voice message telling them exactly why I was calling. I would leave my cell phone and office number, twice. This gave them a chance to find a pen to write it down. I would ask them to give me a call if they needed help getting more applicants to review.

The listings came in. One after the other. The voice messages I left were getting me calls back.

"This is Issa speaking; how can I provide you with world class service?"

"I heard your voice message. I have 52 units and 8 of them are vacant. Can you help me?"

"Sure, let's begin with your full name and the addresses of your apartments."

I kept my head down, dialing numbers, scheduling appointments and listing properties for sale and for rent. By the time I looked up, the month was over. Jessica announced to the team that I had won February's competition, and her message sent shockwaves across the company. Eric always won these competitions until I came along.

At this time my new client Marco, a Wall Street analyst turned real estate investor, introduced me to his ex-boss Kevin. Kevin was a retired multi-millionaire Wall Street executive. Here was a man who had headed up a $40-billion hedge fund. He had years and years of wisdom and experience. Now he was coming to me for advice about his rental business. I can't even begin to describe how much it meant to me that a man of Kevin's stature seemed to think highly of me.

The Story of Betty Ellis

Although I was focusing almost all of my energy on money-making activities, I also had a strong desire to help people find affordable homes where they could be happy and raise their families.

That's why I immediately said, "Yes". when one of the senior agents in our company asked me if I would try to help a woman named Betty Ellis find a house to buy.

Betty was a fifty-three year old African American woman who had a Section 8 government rental voucher worth $925 per month. This was her limit to rent an apartment.

However, there is a provision in federal housing laws which makes it possible for Section 8 recipients to buy their own homes. As long as their monthly payments for their mortgage (principle and interest), insurance and taxes are all within the voucher amount.

Betty Ellis wanted to use her Section 8 voucher to buy a home. She had $925 to spend on it every month. Believe me when I tell you that it is almost impossible to find a home in Northern New Jersey—especially in close proximity to Manhattan—with that budget! If I were going to make this happen, it would require much of my time for very little money. With all the time I would spend, I could rent out a large number of luxury apartments and make a greater return on my time invested. Nevertheless, not everything is about the money. This opportunity reminded me of why I wanted a black shirt at Toys"R"Us.

When I looked into Betty's situation, I discovered that no one had ever been able to buy a house using a Section 8 Voucher in the history of Hudson County. This was attributed to high property values and high taxes. In addition, the process is a pain in the neck! It needed a committed buyer, a committed agent and when we're finally under contract, a committed seller.

I worked my tail off trying to find a decent home that my client could afford. It wasn't easy, but I was determined not to give up—and she felt the same way. Betty was taking classes on mortgage finance, budgeting and credit, learning all about the responsibilities that were going to come her way. She was a determined woman, and I admired her.

CHAPTER 23

MARCH
MADNESS

Betty Ellis

March is a special month in real estate. My office called it March Madness, and it wasn't about college basketball. It was the madness of new real estate inventory coming to the market in droves. Sellers prefer listing their homes in the spring. The weather warms up, flowers blossom, and the smell of the spring season excites homeowners. Additionally, buyers are prepared to embark on their new year homeownership resolutions. The timing couldn't get any better; you had to list or potentially miss out.

The biggest office contest was the March Madness Competition. On March 2, 2011 Steve Jobs made a surprise appearance to announce the new and completely redesigned iPad 2. It was faster, had better battery life and came with 2 cameras, front and rear. It was the hottest tablet on the market and Jessica took full advantage.

Jessica created a point system to reward real estate activity. For example,

5 points for a new listing and 10 points for a fully executed contract.

"This time, whoever gets the most points will win the March Madness Competition and receive an Apple iPad 2!"

The office was buzzing.

"How cool is that?"

"What a productivity tool!"

"Can you imagine showing up to your listing appointment with the iPad 2?"

Some people wanted the iPad, and others were not moved by any competition. I wanted to compete for the adrenaline. I had a family to support, and that was the best way I knew how to do it. I learned that when I compete, the best of me comes out. I'd also happily take the iPad 2.

Okay, let's slow down a second. Winning a listing competition is one thing. You had to focus on literally doing one thing: list. Winning this competition required executed sales contracts and a mix of everything else. It's not the same. I needed to home in on my banking and credit background and everything I'd learned to come even close.

I was doing much better here in Hoboken than I had done in my prior office, but it still wasn't good enough. I was in need of a major breakthrough, and it had to involve more than winning a contest.

I was also frustrated that after looking for nearly two months, I had not found a single home for Betty Ellis to look at, much less put in an offer. I kept in touch with her, and her upbeat attitude kept me going. She knew I was going to find the perfect place for her.

My new friend Vivi came up to me and said, "I've been in this business for years. I admire your hustle and want you to know that I am rooting for you."

"Thanks, Vivi, that's very kind of you. I am working my butt off and need this win for my family."

I was ecstatic and exhausted.

I thought "Maybe I need a break. Sophia's first birthday is coming up on the 28th and we're throwing her a party." But then I whispered to myself, "Stay focused, let's keep adding deals to the board." (Jessica had a board in the breakroom for us to keep track of our points.)

Ten days into the competition and the board was more than half filled. Everyone was going crazy adding their deals. I began to look at how my competitors were doing. Everyone was killing it. I needed to outperform them all.

That's when Vivi came up to me and said, "Eric is after you, Issa. He saw your numbers on the board and is telling everyone he's going to beat you. But don't worry, he's jealous. He used to win all the competitions until you got here and stopped him in his tracks. Now you got Jessica's attention, and he is pissed."

I said, "Thanks for sharing Vivi, but I'm not so worried about that. I will tell you, I am not going to make it easy for him to win. I hope he doesn't take my ambition personally. After all, we're all on the same team."

Vivi insisted, "Oh, it's personal. Trust me, he's already talking bad about you with his little clique. Don't stoop to that. You're a good man."

I wanted nothing to do with drama. I tried to completely shut it out and kept my eyes on real estate transactions. It was an obsession. The more people I helped, the more referrals I got. As long as I stayed on my phone, the system was unstoppable. Some of my heavy rental work began to materialize, and the pay checks reflected it. We were not out of the woods yet, but I was sleeping better. Sophia's birthday party was all paid for in advance, and I was a happy dad.

A week before the competition was over, Vivi asked to speak with me, and she sounded pretty nervous.

"Issa, you need to know this. I don't think you're going to win. Eric is using his partner's points together with his to beat you. If you notice, his partner has nothing on the board. It is clearly two against one. I'm sorry about that. I wanted to warn you."

I appreciated Vivi's heart in trying to look out for me. It was nice to have someone giving me a heads-up on things. This time, I wanted to use this information as my fuel to work harder in the last week before the end of month. I just knew that Eric couldn't touch me, but I was a bit nervous about two people tag-teaming their way to the top. So, I pushed harder.

On March 29, Jessica sent an email to the team:

> Stoked to see the board downstairs totally full…with that said, it will be impossible to tally all deals from the board. Attached please find two forms—one for rentals and one for sales. You must fill out and email to me by March 31st at midnight. No exceptions.

Thank God, my phone was always ringing, and I found it difficult to keep up with voice messages and missed calls. This is a good problem to have in business.

A few days before it was all over, I thoroughly scanned through my phone and email contacts for any possible transactions left behind. I turned several more unfinished conversations into working relationships and kept adding to my sheets.

The last day was here. I recounted all my points. I made sure not one transaction was missing. I had totally forgotten about the iPad 2. It was all about the win. My heart was pounding as I sent Jessica my final list. Later that evening another lease was signed. I updated my sheets and resent them to Jessica minutes before midnight.

A few minutes later, right at the crack of April, Jessica began a suspenseful thread of emails congratulating the top five. She started with fifth place and moved toward number one. The suspense was killing me. When I saw that my name was not announced for the number two spot. I just knew that it all paid off! What a refreshing sensation! There it was "the winner of our March Madness Competition is Issa Musharbash..." Any feelings of being a loser that had been tucked away in the dark corners of my mind vanished. I knew I was born for greatness. This feeling had become somewhat familiar.

Jessica's email went on to say, 'Now that you've won the March Madness Competition, you get to select the rules for April."

After soaking in all the congratulatory emails. I replied back with my gratitude and the rules for April. I got the iPad 2 and had it engraved with the words "All Things are Possible." After that, my focus went right back to work.

We'd had the February contest focused on listings, the March Madness contest on a combination of listings and contracts, including leases, so I thought it was fitting to make the April contest about closings. After all, that's when we actually got paid. The person who could close the most pending files in April and rack up the most points, wins.

Winning two competitions did not immediately translate to more income for my household. My checks were not coming fast enough to keep up with my bills. So I had to keep running as fast as I could go.

I had to keep prospecting, following up on leads, showing properties and presenting at listing appointments. It was an all-or-nothing mindset. I started to see traction and was happy for my performance. Things were finally beginning to turn around.

After applying the same work ethic every single day, I was able to win April, too, and it meant even more. Now I knew there was nothing that could stop me in real estate sales. It became my world! These series of victories allowed me to get my financials in order.

The Merry Months May and June

The month of May was here, and I was so happy. I booked a 4-day trip to the Hard Rock Resort in Punta Cana, Dominican Republic so Ketty and I could celebrate our second wedding anniversary. My mother took good care of Sophia while we were away.

In June, the franchise held an awards dinner, where I was given the Ruby award for my achievements over the last six months. It was a really nice trophy, and I felt honored to receive it, but I also remember thinking, "I wonder what they'd think of me if they knew what my own credit score was." Although my bills were caught up, it would take some time to rebuild my credit profile.

A Home at Last

It was also in June that the impossible happened. I found a nice little home for Betty Ellis. The homeowner was a very nice gentleman who actually cut the price so Ms. Ellis could afford the place.

But there was an issue.

Before a house can be sold, it must undergo a complete state inspection.

This time, the inspector found 17 repairs that needed to be made before the home could be sold.

To my amazement, the homeowner agreed to make all the repairs, without bumping up the selling price of the house. Betty was another step closer to home ownership, but not until we got the home re-inspected.

This time, another 12 items were found that had to be corrected before Betty could take ownership of her new home. I was exasperated because it seemed that the bureaucrats were going to get in the way of my client's dream of home ownership.

The homeowner was a saint. He went to work making the repairs—and the happy day soon came when Betty Ellis was given the keys to her new house at the closing table. I was so happy for her, and I couldn't stop smiling myself. Reporters from the local newspapers showed up that day to record the historic moment for posterity. Our picture was in the paper—and I'll always remember that special moment. To top it off, the CEO of the franchise, who oversees over 100,000 agents worldwide, printed out the news article and mailed it to me with congratulatory remarks on a sticky note.

As I said, this transaction did not make me rich. It was another encouraging moment, reminding me of what I could do if I put my mind to it and refused to give up. For the next few weeks, I suddenly found that I was busier than I had ever been, and, in fact, it was too much for me to handle on my own. I couldn't possibly deal with all the phone calls. Sometimes it took me several days to get back to someone and that was way too long. Potential sales were slipping through the cracks. I was always dealing with 15 or 16 listings at a time—and sometimes more than that. I needed help!

Help!

I'd been telling my brother Hanna and my wife Ketty and a few friends to get their real estate licenses. Hanna did first. He would take all the showings, while I focused on listings. I also asked my friend Anthony to come work for me. He began keeping track of calls, managing our calendars and otherwise organizing our day. Both of them were a tremendous help to me.

Although Hanna was working hard, I wanted to make sure he had all the training he needed. So, one night I decided to shadow him when he went out to show some rentals to prospective clients.

As usual, we were dressed up with suits and ties. We went to an apartment on 19th Street in Bayonne, and met a young woman named Priscilla who was interested in renting it. In the course of our conversation, I asked her what she did for a living.

"I'm a property manager for a brand-new Australian-based Company that buys, repairs and leases properties. I'm in charge of the leasing team—and man, it's busy."

"Do you have a lot of vacancies?"

"Oh, yeah. We have at least 40 vacancies right now and every week we're buying a number of properties."

"Well, why don't you give me an opportunity to work with you and help you with those vacancies. We've been killing it with sales and rentals."

She shook her head, "My agency doesn't like to work with real estate agents." She went on to tell me how so many agents lose keys, act irresponsible, become difficult to manage and create other problems.

I smiled and said, "Well, we're not like that. How many times have you seen two agents show up dressed in suits, just to show an apartment?"

She nodded, "I'll have to admit, I was impressed when you two showed up in suits."

"My heart shakes every time I learn of a unit that's vacant for too long, it's a big problem. It costs you a lot of money. Why don't you give us a shot at filling those empty apartments?"

She thought about it for a moment and said, "Well, the least I can do is talk to my boss. Let's connect in a week."

I called a week later and asked if they still had 40 vacancies. Priscilla laughed, "No, we have over 60 now."

When I asked about her boss, she said she hadn't yet been able to talk to him because he'd been on the road. He was back in town, now, and she'd give him a call. True to her word, she called back an hour or so later and said we had a meeting for the following Tuesday morning. I was so excited, I had to restrain myself from dancing around the room.

No Time to Lose

It was a short dance. I had to get ready for our meeting and didn't have much time. Consequently, I asked a few friends to help us.

One of the most important things we did was put together a map of Jersey City, with markers showing where all of the vacant apartments were located. Many of them were in the same area, which meant that we could show a prospective tenant several properties in a single afternoon. If he or she didn't like the first place we showed, we could move on to the second, third and so on.

Naturally, this would increase our chances of getting applications. As it turned out, Priscilla's boss agreed with us, and we walked out of that meeting with 60-70 listings! We felt that we had won a great victory. And so we had!

I couldn't wait to tell Ketty what had happened. Like me, she was excited, and so proud of our accomplishments. Her encouragement and appreciation at that moment meant more than I can explain.

As I thought about where my life was going, I couldn't help but think back to those difficult days I had gone through when I first came to America. I could see the tormented little boy who cried himself to sleep at night after being bullied all day at school, simply because he was different—a foreigner with a big nose. I remembered the pain of being hit, kicked and beaten—and even worse, the pain of being called names and told, "Go back to your country."

Through hard work, perseverance and God's grace, I had come such a long, long way. Tears of gratitude filled my eyes, and I said a silent prayer for all the others who were walking the long, difficult road I had walked. I prayed that they would have the perseverance and strength they needed to see their dreams come into existence.

CHAPTER 24

THE
FIRE

New Office

I began organizing myself with the intent to start my own real estate firm. I mistakenly believed that the law required me to be a salesperson for at least three years before I was allowed to open my own brokerage.

When I spoke with my client Marco, who had since become a friend, he told me I had it wrong.

"You can open your business any time; you need three years to be the broker." Then he urged, "You don't have to be the broker yet; you can hire a broker for your company."

When I looked into the matter further, I discovered he was right. There was nothing standing in my way. As a result, I began searching for an office, but I felt like I was doing something wrong. Here I was working at a good company and yet planning to leave when I found an affordable office space. What a conflict I was having within!

To make matters worse, the owners of my current company honored me and other 2011 top producers with unprecedented billboard ads posted all over the Hoboken and Jersey City PATH stations. If you made it on a billboard, you begin to feel a greater sense of accomplishment. Yet, there I was trying to throw all of this away and start from scratch, again.

In the noise of billboards, my desire to remain faded away, and I was ready to launch with a new clarity. Having spent the last 20 months in the business, from nearly quitting to breaking through, I wanted to leverage this experience to prepare others coming into the business. With Ketty's encouragement again, I took another leap of faith. This time, it was opening our own real estate brokerage and it had to be less about us, maybe bigger than us. And so, we did not want to name it after a person. It had to outlast us and generations to come, so we called it Provident Legacy Real Estate Services. Against the advice of the masses, we went head-on.

Fire!

Shortly after we had signed a 10-year lease on our new location, some construction workers accidentally touched off a fire in our building that resulted in heavy smoke and water damage to the floors, walls and ceiling of our new office.

My client Kevin, the multi-millionaire Wall Street wizard, saw it as a sign that I was moving too fast.

"Perhaps this is a sign from the gods that you need to reverse course," he said. "You're still young. Maybe you need to get some more experience before you step out and try to make your mark."

As much as I respected Kevin and valued his advice, I decided that I couldn't turn back.

Although he was firm in his opinion, there was a greater voice inside me.

My dream wasn't about building my own kingdom, but rather about maximizing the impact I could have on agents, who in turn help me service the clients. In order to do this right, I felt that I had to step out and start this firm.

Holding on to the Dream

The dream I had was worth whatever risk it took to make it come true. If I failed, I'd just pick myself up and start all over. If my family went through some tough times—well, we'd been there before, and Ketty and I knew that we'd come out the other side better than ever.

As it turned out, the fire was yet another blessing in disguise.

Because of the repairs that were made after the fire, we wound up getting a brand-new office. It was much nicer than the original office, but because I had signed a 10-year lease, the price did not go up. As it turned out, Provident Legacy quickly outgrew that office, and we have been subletting it since. What's more, we've been receiving the current value of the office in rent, while paying the rent we negotiated nearly 9 years ago. What looked like a major loss has turned out to be a benefit to us for 10 years. That's a small example of the sort of things that happen when you hold on to your dreams and anchor them to your faith long enough. It's what happens when you pour your heart and soul into chasing your dreams in the face of rejection and opposition.

As I thought about how to conclude my book, I wanted it to be about you. How can my story become yours? So, I have a few questions for you. Take your time to writing the answers down. Do not move to the next question until you've written down the answer to the previous one.

1. What are your dreams? Write them down.

2. Are there any more? If so, write those down, too.

3. What stands in the way of your dreams?

4. Can you be more specific?

5. Is fear involved? If so, describe how.

6. What anchors do you have that can hold your dreams in place when storms of life come?

7. How can you face opposition to your dreams?

8. What will it cost you to face what stands between you and your dreams?

9. Are you willing to pay the price?

10. Why?

11. Now, why is the answer to question #10 important to you?

Ok, enough questions. Although I don't intend to turn this into a self-help section of the book, I do sincerely want you to reflect on your own story. I wrote mine as openly as I can, showing you the pain and joy of achieving dreams in hope of encouraging you to go wild after your dreams. And if you're already a dreamer, like me, activate new dreams. As you do, I hope you find the courage to share your journey with me and others.

EPILOGUE

The story is far from over. It continues through the day-to-day activities of the company I founded in 2012, Provident Legacy, and the life I choose to lead. In some ways, what you have been reading so far is just the prologue for what has happened and continues to happen, since Provident Legacy opened its doors. Today, Ketty and I are raising three beautiful children. After Sophia came Abraham. After Abraham, came Joseph. I aspire to share these amazing stories with you in future writings.

Recently, people have asked me to write about starting up a business. Since there are countless books on that topic, I thought I'd briefly share with you what I had to do before launching a business, which ironically continues to guide my business.

At the start of the new year in 2012, I sat down and thoroughly thought through what my values had become. I wanted to know if those values could govern the decisions and the direction of the company I wanted to start. I've searched myself and what I had learned over the years from people I admired and began shaping our company's core values.

Here they are:

1-Integrity of Character:

Before our gifts and abilities, we first uphold our character. Our character is the most important part of doing business. We believe that our gifts and abilities can only take us as far as our character can sustain us.

2-Leadership and Accountability:

We lead by example and hold ourselves accountable. We believe that accountability is one of the greatest nutrients for healthy growth in leadership. We strive to lead our associates and clients with an excellent blend of professional will and personal humility.

3-Diversity and Inclusion:

We value our differences and make certain each associate has a seat at the table, ensuring diversity and inclusion in the opportunities we seize.

4-Empowerment and Performance:

We believe in the tremendous power that is within our associates. We diligently strive to see our associates pull from within to deliver breakthrough results for our clients.

5-World-Class Delivery:

Service is at the heart of everything we do. We aspire to serve our clients with the highest level of care possible; and when we get there, we'll push the bar higher.

These core values remain today as our moral compass. They have served us well, especially when making vital decisions. When things are gray, our core values help turn them into black or white.

I am thankful that my life experiences have shaped me into who I am. They've instilled values that inform the decisions we make at work and at home.

Under the guidance of these values, we continue to innovate and impact our industry, locally and regionally. God willing, one day the impact will spread nationally and internationally.

Every year, our associates nominate five award recipients, one representing each core value. These awards hold more treasure than any sales awards, because our core value awards represent who we are while our sales awards recognize only what we've accomplished. I find it more meaningful to do from a place of being, rather than to be from a place of doing.

As we conclude our time together, I wanted to leave you with the following letter that I wrote to the 12-year-old boy you read about in Chapter 1. As I wrote this letter, it helped me heal some wounds. Perhaps I may never heal completely from the scars of my past, but a little bit of pain is a good reminder of the road I've traveled. You have a story, too. Go ahead, tell it.

To: 12-year-old Issa

Bayonne, New Jersey

Dear Issa,

I commend your hustle and long-range view of life. Perhaps at the age of 12, you should be in sports, playing soccer with your friends on weekends and developing as a goalkeeper. Who knows, maybe channeling all of your efforts into the game would have turned you into a professional soccer player. Instead, you ignored your childhood possibilities because you had your mother on your mind. Thank you for honoring her with your work ethic early in your youth. Your sacrifices have already blessed her more than you know and will provide her with much needed hope during your dark teenage years.

If I can ask you to do something for yourself immediately, it's to speak up and share your concerns. Don't let anything that bothers you sit unresolved in your heart and mind. Talk about it with a trusted friend and remember that you always have a true friend in your mother.

Now, listen to me closely. Having a stepdad does not make your own dad less important. Your dad will be okay without you, but you will not be okay without a dad. Your stepfather works endless hours driving a taxi in New York City to keep a roof over your head. Try talking to him and see what's in his heart. I promise you, it's gold. I know you're going to struggle to call him dad for a while and that's okay. Nonetheless, I want you to know that one day, your children will naturally and gladly call him grandpa.

Do not take your bond with your siblings lightly. The bond you're building now will result in rewarding relationships decades later. Certainly, you'll all move on to build your own lives and start new families. Still, that bond will keep you close no matter how far apart you travel.

Lastly, when people hurt you, forgive them. If they hurt you again, forgive them more. I've seen what you've been through. Don't take rejection personally. It's usually done out of ignorance instead of truth. If people knew where you've been and where you're going, their perspectives would change. You'll always have haters, so don't try to please everyone. Do what is right, even if it's not popular. Remember that your freedom will be tied to genuine forgiveness. When you think that they do not deserve your forgiveness, reconsider. Just remember that forgiveness is less about them and more about you. Trust that process; it not only heals, it releases you to greatness. Hold on to your faith, not just until the struggle is over or when your dreams come true. Hold on to it dearly until the end.

ACKNOWLEDGMENTS

Writing a book is truly a miraculous process and requires so much effort by so many amazing individuals. The acknowledgment section of this book feels like a drop in the ocean when I think about the ceaseless support and extraordinary love poured into it by many collaborators. I am profoundly grateful to all of you.

To friends who participated in focus groups, read the manuscript in different stages of its development and provided much needed wisdom, clarity and ideas: Amanda Abdelsayed, Ana Colon, Christopher Gasca, Dana Cadena, Elias Rodriguez, Francine Mikhail, Helen Kerins, John Corpening, Josue Sanchez, Mayan Alena Hein, Peter Lopez, Rev. Cleo Santiago, Rossana Mirabel, Rozani Penteado, Sabrina Perez, Sami Saad, Sheetal Sawhney, Victor Llerena and Victoria Llerena. You have all warmed my heart with your contributions, and I am greatly appreciative of you.

To David Wimbish, who served as my developmental editor and devoted endless hours to this project, you've earned a special place in my heart.

To my Harvard writing instructor, Jerusha Achterberg, MPH, thank you for sweeping through my book one last time before print and uncovering opportunities to enhance, just as you've done with all my papers in class. I am profoundly grateful for your service.

To Mayan Alena Hein, I could not have asked for a better book-launch manager. Your sleepless nights have not gone unnoticed and your labor was not in vain. Thank you for believing in this project and choosing to do meaningful work.

To Sabrina Perez and Pastor Sergio Revelli, thank you for teaming up and making this book available in español. Your gifts and talents were relentlessly poured into this project, and words can not express how deeply I appreciate and love you! Thank you for allowing me to reach the amazing and resilient Spanish-reading people of the world!

To Dr. Carlos Hernandez, who am I that you would invest your limited and valuable time to review my work, provide extensive feedback on it and eventually, write the foreword? This is truly a dream come true and I am forever indebted to you.

To Bishop Joshua Rodriguez and Pastor Paula Rodriguez, you were sent from heaven to disrupt my path. Thank you for the nearly two decades of mentorship, guiding me from a teenager in darkness to a beautiful family life with my wife and kids. Your authenticity is contagious, and your consistency is paramount. To The Cityline Church leadership and congregation, I will forever remain grateful.

To Peter Lopez, for planting the seed to write this book. To Tyler Wagner and the Authors Unite team for pushing the message forward. To Robert Lee, thank you for taking that back cover photo; my wife and I appreciate you very much.

To Sam Mikhail, for believing in this work and pushing me to finish all aspects of it with your crazy deadlines. I can't continue without acknowledging your entire team, David Leonard, Leslie Victori, Emily Davis, Adia Atwell and Francine Mikhail. In an age of countless marketers, very few read manuscripts and believe in the work; instead, it's a strict algorithm game with no care for quality of content. But you, my friend, and your team are believers. If you don't believe in it, you don't make time for it. In my opinion, that's what makes the best marketers. Thank you for making time for this project and going above and beyond.

To my beloved partners Giselle Llerena, Jacob Musharbash, Hanna Musharbash and Duda Penteado, thank you for holding it down and leading by example, especially in my absence. You are truly the embodiment of Provident Legacy's core values. Together, you are my greatest desire in leading an organization. Your passion, love, care and service are pillars of strength for our family of companies. I love you all!

To our wonderful agents and staff at Provident Legacy, thank you for giving me space to get this work done and trusting in our amazing leadership team for guidance and direction. Your story is an extension of mine and there are not enough words I can use to describe how valuable you are to me and my family.

To my mother Lidia, you are my Hero. You are the Hero of this book. You have shown me that true strength comes from kneeling down to our Father in heaven. Your faith continues to inspire me every day. I love you dearly. To my biological father, Isam Musharbash, and stepfather, Gamal Salama, I love you both from a deep place in my heart.

To my siblings, Jacob Musharbash, Hanna Musharbash, Mariana Musharbash, my half-brothers, Melad Salama, Yousef Musharbash and Farah Musharbash and to my step-siblings, Fadee Salama, Shadee Salama, Heba Salama and Doaa Salama, I love you guys. The manner in which our family was blended must have been the work of angels. People still ask me, even unto this day, how do we keep a cordial and loving relationship as a blended family? My answer, you're all awesome! To all my siblings-in-law, Victor, Giselle, Vicky, Laura, George, Mary and Lucia, I love you all too!

To my wife, Ketty Musharbash, my first girlfriend and the love of my life, thank you for your endless support and push to get this story out. There is no way I could have fathomed the idea of doing this without you. You are the sunshine of my life. We have seen all kinds of seasons in our marriage, seasons of difficulties and lack and seasons of great joy and abundance. In all seasons, you have been firmly standing by my side. Even in failure, you find the right words to remind me of how deeply committed you are to our future. You are my best friend. Thank you for being a pillar in our home and an exemplary mother to our children.

And last, but certainly not least, to my children, Sophia, Abraham and Joseph, you are the reason I wrote this book. You are all smart and unique. You are beautiful and strong. I am so proud to be your father. Nothing makes me happier than watching you grow and become all that God has destined for you to be. But I write to you with caution. You are living in the luxuries that your father never had. Do not let the comfort of life rob you of a desire to achieve great things. I hope this book reminds you of the journey that brought you here and inspires you to fight for your dreams. Achieving your dreams will not be easy, but if you set your mind to them and anchor yourself to your faith in God, nothing can stop you. I promise. I love you dearly. Go out and win!